Favorites from the Editors of AMERICAN PATCHWORK & QUILTING®

# Quilting with Precuts

### 31 FUN & EASY PROJECTS
### WITH FAT QUARTERS, FAT EIGHTHS,
### STRIPS & SQUARES

A Better Homes and Gardens® Book

An Imprint of

HMH

Published by:
**Houghton Mifflin Harcourt**
Boston • New York
www.hmhbooks.com

For information about permission to reproduce selections from this book, write to Permissions, Houghton Mifflin Harcourt Publishing Company, 215 Park Avenue South, New York, New York 10003.

www.hmhbooks.com

Library of Congress Control Number available from the publisher upon request.
ISBN: 978-1-118-45109-0 (pbk)

Printed in the United States of America

DOR 10 9 8 7 6 5 4 3 2 1

# introduction

*delicious!* Is there any better word to describe the delightful assortment of precut fabrics you find at your local quilt shop? The yummy array of colors and prints are not just eye candy—they're tactile, too. How often do you find yourself running your fingers over the smooth edges of a roll of precut strips or peeling back the corners of a fat-quarter bundle for a better look at the prints?

Precut shapes and sizes range from fat quarters and fat eighths to skinny strips and squares large and small. But they all share one common thread: They provide the perfect way to jump-start a quilt project.

Starting with precut pieces gives you an instant assortment of fabrics that look great together. You also gain the time-saving advantage of working with manageable, quick-to-cut fabric pieces.

So whether you sort through your stash or make a run to the quilt store to stock up on precuts, get ready to piece together these fun projects. Mmmm, they're good!

# contents

## departments

## fat quarters & fat eighths

## strips

## squares

# fat quarters
## &
# fat eighths

# flowerSHOW

Florals and solids combine for a stunning but easy-to-sew bed quilt. You can change the theme of the large rectangles— think plaids or reproduction prints—to customize any room.

DESIGNERS **BILL KERR AND WEEKS RINGLE OF FUN QUILTS** (funquilts.com)

## materials

- 11—18×22" pieces (fat quarters) or 2¾ yards total assorted florals (pieced rows)
- ½ yard solid red (pieced rows)
- 4⅜ yards solid white (sashing, border)
- ¾ yard solid orange (binding)
- 6 yards backing fabric
- 75×107" batting

Finished quilt: 67×98½"

**Quantities** are for 44/45"-wide, 100% cotton fabrics. **Measurements** include ¼" seam allowances. Sew with right sides together unless otherwise stated.

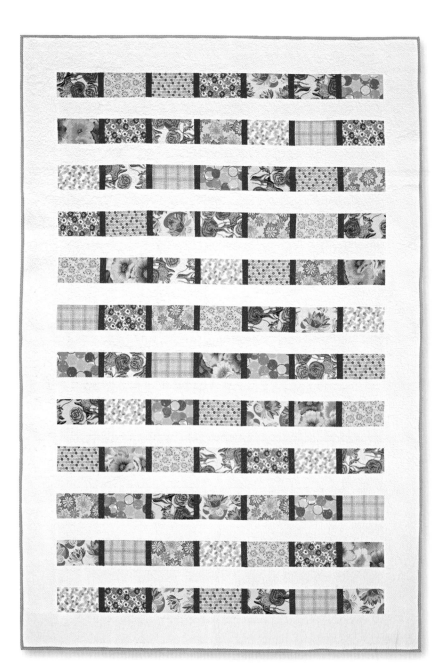

## cut fabrics

Cut pieces in the following order. Cut sashing and border strips lengthwise (parallel to the selvages).

**From each assorted floral fat quarter, cut:**
- 8—4½×7½" rectangles (you will use 84 of the 88 total cut)

**From solid red, cut:**
- 72—1½×4½" rectangles

**From solid white, cut:**
- 2—6¼×87" border strips
- 2—6¼×67" border strips
- 11—4×55½" sashing strips

**From solid orange, cut:**
- 9—2½×42" binding strips

## pressing method

For more accurate sewing, designers Bill Kerr and Weeks Ringle press all seams open, allowing for precise seam alignment and easy pinning through seams.

Before pressing a seam open, set the seam. To set a seam, press the seam as it was sewn, without opening the fabric pieces. This helps meld or sink the stitches into the fabric, leaving you with a less bulky seam allowance after you press it open.

## assemble pieced rows

Referring to **Quilt Assembly Diagram**, sew together seven assorted floral 4½×7½" rectangles and six solid red 1½×4½" rectangles to make a pieced row; press seams open. The pieced row should be 4½×55½" including seam allowances. Repeat to make 12 pieced rows total.

## assemble quilt top

**1** Referring to **Quilt Assembly Diagram**, lay out pieced rows and solid white 4×55½" sashing strips in 23 rows.

**2** Sew together rows and sashing strips to make quilt center. Press seams open. The quilt center should be 55½×87" including seam allowances.

**3** Add solid white 6¼×87" border strips to long edges of quilt center. Sew solid white 6¼×67" border strips to remaining edges to complete quilt top. Press all seams open.

## finish quilt

**1** Layer quilt top, batting, and backing; baste. (For details, see Complete Quilt, *page 175*.)

**2** Quilt as desired. Weeks machine-quilted a swirl motif across the quilt top.

**3** Bind with solid orange binding strips. (For details, see Complete Quilt.)

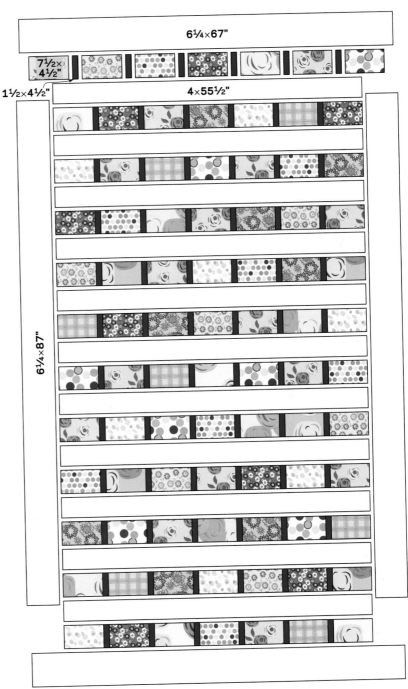

QUILT ASSEMBLY DIAGRAM

# HOT
# tamale

DESIGNER **EMILY OWENS OF TESSUTI ZOO** (tessutizoo.com)

This quilt is sizzling hot and super simple. If you can cut a strip and sew a seam, you can make this throw in a heartbeat.

## materials

- 12—18×22" pieces (fat quarters) or 2 yards total assorted bright prints, florals, stripes, and polka dots (pieced rows)
- 1⅝ yards purple print (sashing, border)
- ½ yard green print (binding)
- 3 yards backing fabric
- 53×68" batting

Finished quilt: 44½×59½"

Quantities are for 44/45"-wide, 100% cotton fabrics. Measurements include ¼" seam allowances. Sew with right sides together unless otherwise stated.

## cut fabrics

Cut pieces in the following order. Cut sashing and border strips lengthwise (parallel to the selvages).

**From assorted bright prints, florals, stripes, and polka dots, cut:**

- 40—4×6" rectangles
- 50—3×6" rectangles

**From purple print, cut:**

- 6—3¼×53½" sashing strips
- 2—3½×44½" border strips

**From green print, cut:**

- 6—2½×42" binding strips

## assemble pieced rows

Referring to **Quilt Assembly Diagram** and photo, *opposite*, sew together eight assorted bright print, floral, stripe, and polka dot 4×6" rectangles and 10 assorted 3×6" rectangles to make a pieced row; press seams in one direction. The pieced row should be 6×53½" including seam allowances. Repeat to make five pieced rows total.

## assemble quilt top

1 Referring to **Quilt Assembly Diagram,** lay out pieced rows and purple print 3¼×53½" sashing strips in 11 rows.

2 Sew together pieced rows and strips. Press seams toward sashing strips.

3 Join purple print 3½×44½" border strips to top and bottom edges to complete quilt top. Press seams toward border.

## finish quilt

1 Layer quilt top, batting, and backing; baste. (For details, see Complete Quilt, *page 175*.)

2 Quilt as desired. Machine-quilter Connie Haile stitched an allover meandering pattern across the quilt top.

3 Bind with green print binding strips. (For details, see Complete Quilt.)

# COLOR OPTION

Need a quick gift for a special someone? Switch out the fabrics in *Hot Tamale* with red-and-white prints for a super sweet throw. These vintage-inspired prints sparkle when mixed with complementary fabrics.

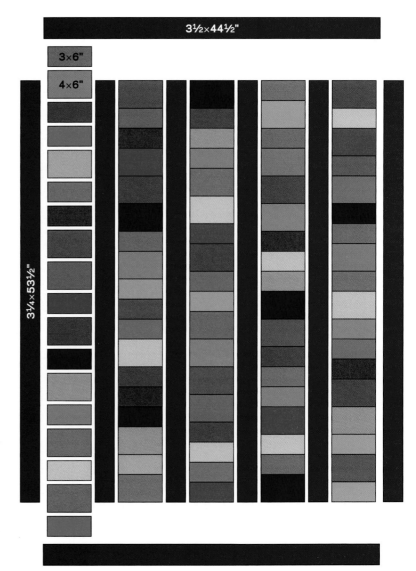

**QUILT ASSEMBLY DIAGRAM**

··· **tip** ···

*If your ruler slips when you put pressure on it, adhere small sandpaper dots*
*to its underside. Self-adhesive sandpaper dots are available at quilt shops, or you*
*can make your own with a hole punch, fine-grain sandpaper, and glue.*

Reproduction prints commemorating Abraham Lincoln's birth get center stage in a strikingly simple arrangement that has the look of an antique quilt.

DESIGNER **AMY WALSH OF BLUE UNDERGROUND STUDIOS**
(blueundergroundstudios.com)

# lincoln's
# PLATFORM

## materials

- 8—18×22" pieces (fat quarters) *or* 2 yards total assorted cream prints (blocks)
- 10—18×22" pieces (fat quarters) *or* 2½ yards total assorted dark prints in brick red, gray-blue, blue, sage green, and chocolate brown (blocks, setting squares)
- ½ yard dark blue print (binding)
- 3¼ yards backing fabric
- 59×68" batting

Finished quilt: 50½×59½"
Finished block: 3½×5"

Quantities are for 44/45"-wide, 100% cotton fabrics. Measurements include ¼" seam allowances. Sew with right sides together unless otherwise stated.

## cut fabrics

Cut pieces in the following order. See **Cutting Diagrams**, *page 18*, to get the most pieces from each fat quarter.

**From *each* assorted cream print fat quarter, refer to Cutting Diagram A and cut:**
- 20—1¾×4" rectangles (you will use 150 of the 160 total cut)
- 20—1¾×3" rectangles (you will use 150 of the 160 total cut)

**From *each* assorted dark print fat quarter, refer to Cutting Diagram B and cut:**
- 8—5½" setting squares (you will use 75 of the 80 total cut)
- 8—1½×3" rectangles (you will use 75 of the 80 total cut)

**From dark blue print, cut:**
- 6—2½×42" binding strips

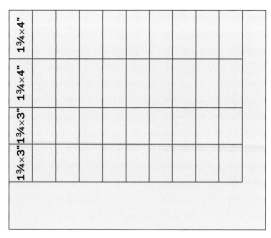

CUTTING DIAGRAM A    CUTTING DIAGRAM B

## assemble blocks

**1** Referring to **Block Assembly Diagram,** sew together two matching cream print 1¾×3" rectangles and one assorted dark print 1½×3" rectangle to make a pieced row. Press seams toward dark print rectangle.

**BLOCK ASSEMBLY DIAGRAM**

**2** Add two matching cream print 1¾×4" rectangles to long edges of pieced row to complete block. Press seams away from pieced row. The block should be 4×5½" including seam allowances.

**3** Repeat steps 1 and 2 to make 75 blocks total.

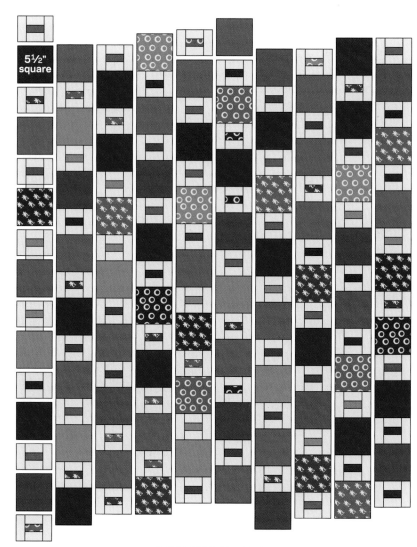

**QUILT ASSEMBLY DIAGRAM**

*Periodically remove the blade from your rotary cutter and carefully wipe away any lint and residue. Take the cutter apart, one piece at a time, laying out the parts in order. Add one drop of sewing machine oil around the center of the blade before reassembling the cutter.*

## assemble quilt top

**1** Referring to **Quilt Assembly Diagram**, lay out blocks and 75 assorted dark print 5½" setting squares in 10 vertical rows. Designer Amy Walsh aligned the blocks so the bottom right corner and the top left corner of adjacent blocks meet diagonally. The rows will be uneven when pieced together; you will trim them later.

**2** Sew together pieces in each vertical row. Press seams toward setting squares. Join vertical rows; press seams open.

**3** Referring to **Trim Diagram**, trim top and bottom edges of vertical rows to square up edges and complete quilt top. The trimmed quilt top should be 50½×59½" including seam allowances.

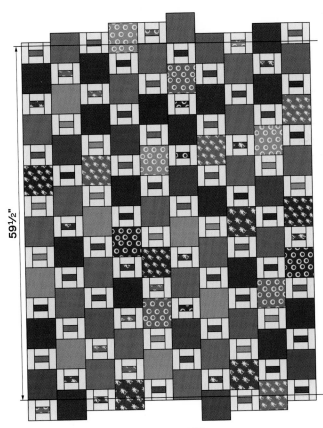

TRIM DIAGRAM

## finish quilt

1 Layer quilt top, batting, and backing; baste. (For details, see Complete Quilt, *page 175*.)

2 Quilt as desired. Designer Amy Walsh machine-quilted her project in an allover meandering stitch using tan thread. She chose this option because she wanted the quilting to add texture to her project without interfering with the pieced design.

3 Bind with dark blue print binding strips. (For details, see Complete Quilt.)

## COLOR OPTION

If reproduction fabrics aren't your style, select contemporary prints to make *Lincoln's Platform* your way. Quiltmaker Kathleen Williams chose a subtle teal check to surround the strong colors of the blue, green, and chocolate prints in her calming throw.

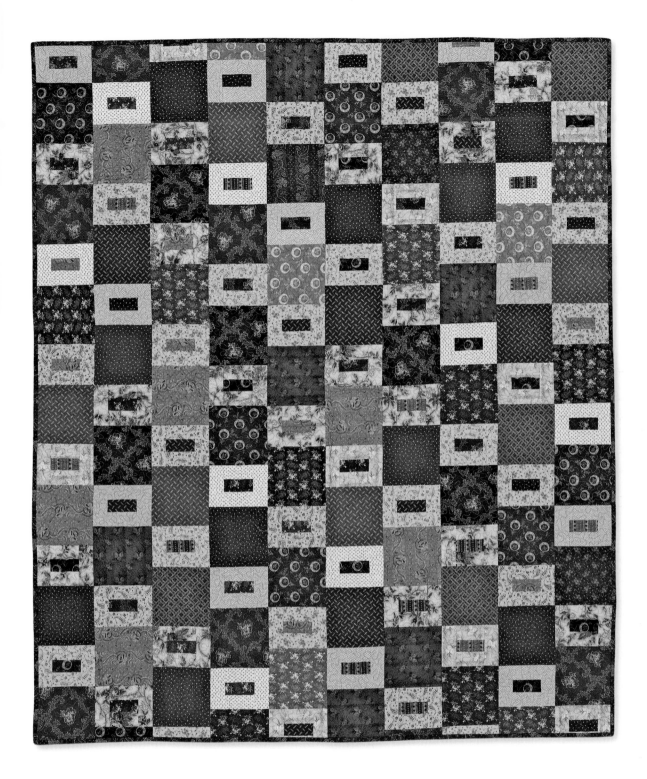

··· tip ···

*Begin each project with a new sewing machine needle,*
*or change it after every eight hours of sewing. A blunt needle*
*can weaken fabric or cause skipped stitches.*

# brick by brick

Finish this quilt of "bricks" quickly using just one shape and 29 complementary fat quarters from one collection or your stash.

## materials

- 24—18×22" pieces* (fat quarters) assorted prints in green, white, pink, yellow, orange, and gray (rectangles)
  * We used 4 fat quarters of each color
- 5—18×22" pieces* (fat quarters) assorted prints (binding)
  * We used 4 white print fat quarters and 1 green print fat quarter for binding
- 5⅓ yards backing fabric
- 81×96" batting

Finished quilt: 72½×88"

Quantities are for 44/45"-wide, 100% cotton fabrics. Measurements include ¼" seam allowances. Sew with right sides together unless otherwise stated.

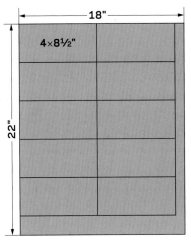

**CUTTING DIAGRAM**

## cut fabrics

Cut fabrics in the following order. See **Cutting Diagram** to cut the most 4×8½" rectangles from each fat quarter.

**From *each* assorted green, white, pink, yellow, orange, and gray print fat quarter, cut:**
- 10—4×8½" rectangles (you will use 237 of the 240 total rectangles cut)

**From *each* assorted print fat quarter, cut:**
- 4—2½×22" binding strips

## assemble quilt top

1  Referring to **Quilt Assembly Diagram**, sew together nine assorted green, white, pink, yellow, orange, or gray print 4×8½" rectangles in a row to make strip A. Press seams open. Strip A should be 4×72½" including seam allowances. Repeat to make 13 A strips total.

2  Sew together 10 assorted green, white, pink, yellow, orange, or gray print 4×8½" rectangles in a row to make strip B. Press seams open. Repeat to make 12 B strips total.

3  Fold one strip A in half crosswise to find center of strip; mark. Repeat to mark center of each strip A.

4  Lay out strips on a design wall or floor, alternating strips A and B, until you are pleased with the color arrangement of the rectangles.

5  Fold one strip B in half crosswise to find center of strip; mark **(Trimming Diagram)**. Using an acrylic ruler and rotary cutter, trim strip B 4¼" from last seam on each end. The trimmed strip B should be 4×72½" including seam allowances. Repeat to mark center and trim ends of each strip B. (To avoid confusion, return each strip B to its place on the design wall before removing another.)

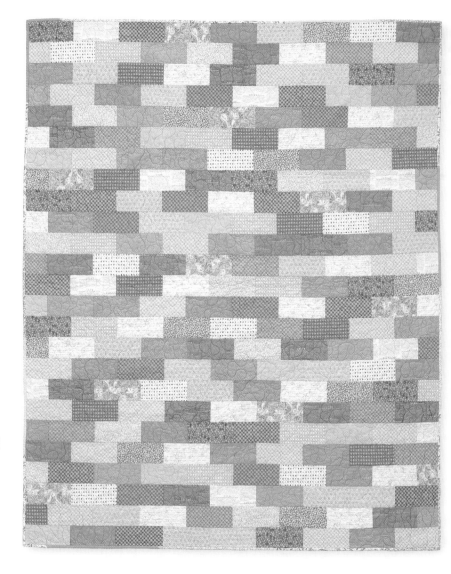

6  Aligning center marks and matching raw ends, sew together A and B strips to complete quilt top. Press seams in one direction.

## finish quilt

1  Layer quilt top, batting, and backing; baste. (For details, see Complete Quilt, *page 175.*)

2  Quilt as desired. Nancy Sharr machine-quilted continuous loops across the quilt top.

3  Using diagonal seams, sew together assorted print 2½×22" binding strips to make a pieced binding strip. Bind quilt with pieced binding strip. (For details, see Complete Quilt.)

center

4¼"    4¼"

**TRIMMING DIAGRAM**

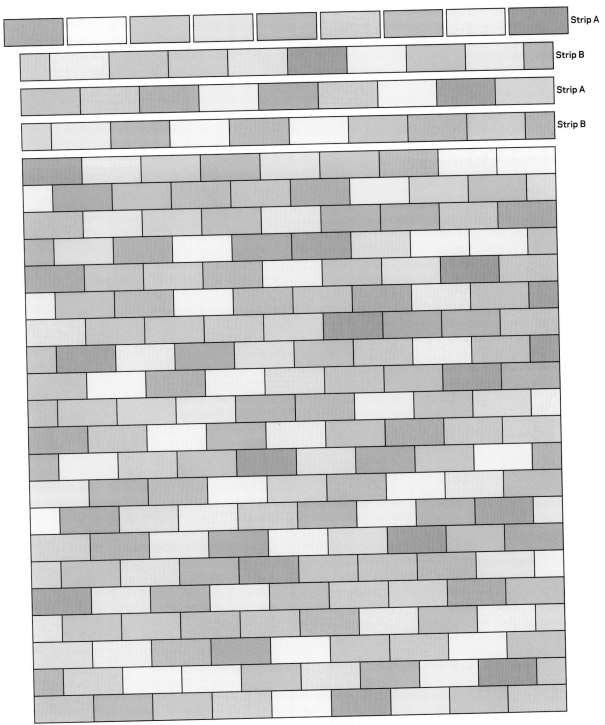

Strip A

Strip B

Strip A

Strip B

QUILT ASSEMBLY DIAGRAM

# star
# power

Discover the "crazy" way to make stars—
no precise matching points and no paper
piecing. Just layer fat quarters, cut through
all of them at once, and shuffle the deck
to easily create stunning stars.

DESIGNERS **JANET NESBITT** AND **PAM SOLIDAY OF THE BUGGY BARN**
(buggybarnquilts.com)

# learn the crazy way

Just stack, cut, shuffle, and sew. No worries about exact seam allowances either! Trim the blocks when you're finished.

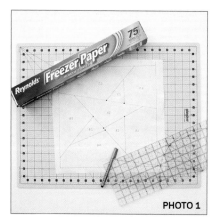

PHOTO 1

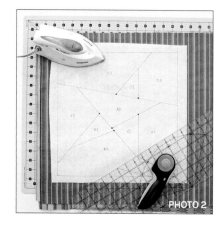

PHOTO 2

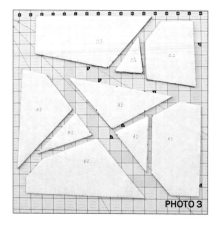

PHOTO 3

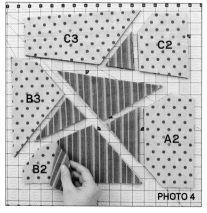

PHOTO 4

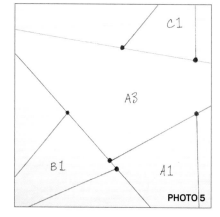

PHOTO 5

## materials

- 13—18×22" pieces (fat quarters) or 2¼ yards total assorted prints in blue, red, green, and gold (blocks, sashing)
- 1⅝ yards brown check (sashing)
- ⅞ yard red floral (setting and corner triangles)
- 1⅛ yards brown dot (border)
- ⅝ yard red tone-on-tone (binding)
- 4 yards backing fabric
- 72" square batting
- Freezer paper

**Finished quilt:** 63⅝" square
**Finished block:** 9" square

**Quantities** are for 44/45"-wide, 100% cotton fabrics.
**Measurements** include ¼" seam allowances. Sew with right sides together unless otherwise stated.

## cut fabrics

Cut pieces in the order that follows in each section.

To plan this quilt in your own colorway, use the **Coloring Diagram** on *Pattern Sheet 2*.

**From brown check, cut:**
- 36—4½×9½" rectangles for sashing
- 12—4½" squares for sashing

**From red floral, cut:**
- 2—14" squares, cutting each diagonally twice in an X for 8 large setting triangles total
- 2—7¼" squares, cutting each in half diagonally for 4 corner triangles total
- 3—7" squares, cutting each diagonally twice in an X for 12 small setting triangles total

**From brown dot, cut:**
- 7—4½×42" strips for border

**From red tone-on-tone, cut:**
- 7—2½×42" binding strips

## cut and prepare block pieces

The **Cutting Template** is in two sections on *Pattern Sheet 1*. To make a full-size Cutting Template, overlap shaded areas and trace both sections on one large sheet of paper.

1 Lay freezer paper shiny side down over full-size Cutting Template. Use a pencil to trace template, tracing all lines, letters, numbers, and dots. Trim freezer-paper Cutting Template roughly ½" beyond outside drawn square **(Photo 1)**.

2 Stack the 13 assorted print fat quarters right sides up, aligning selvage edges and left-hand edges. There should be contrast between adjacent fat quarters because in the completed project each print will be in a block with the prints above and below it. There also must be contrast between the first and last fabrics in the stack.

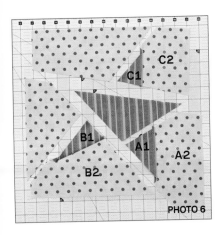

PHOTO 6

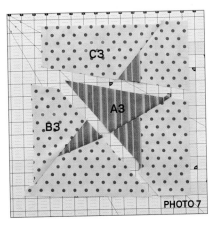

PHOTO 7

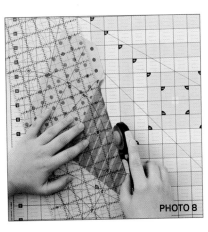

PHOTO 8

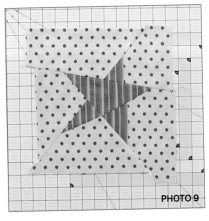

PHOTO 9

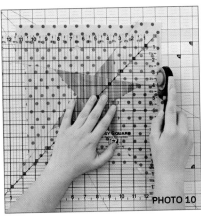

PHOTO 10

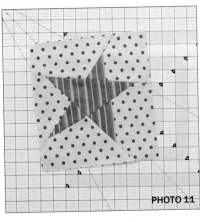

PHOTO 11

**3** Position freezer-paper Cutting Template shiny side down on stacked fat quarters. (You will need fat-quarter fabric scraps to cut remaining pieces, so place template in one corner of the stack, about 1" from edges.) Using a hot, dry iron, press template onto top fat quarter (Photo 2); let cool.

**4** Using a large, sharp rotary cutter with cutting mat and acrylic ruler, press firmly on stack and cut through freezer-paper template and all fat quarters on outside drawn square.

**5** Beginning with section C and working backward, cut template and fat-quarter stack apart on lines separating sections A, B, and C. Then cut on remaining lines to separate sections into three stacks each (Photo 3).

**6** Remove freezer paper from stacked fabric pieces (see organizing tip on *page 32*). Shuffle top fabric piece from

A2, B2, B3, C2, and C3 to bottom of each respective stack (Photo 4).

## about the method
Designers Pam Soliday and Janet Nesbitt created this star block with their improvisational "crazy" method. You'll sew together pieces in sections A, B, and C; join sections into blocks; then square up blocks.

As you join pieces, try to keep inside seams straight, putting extra fabric toward outside edge. Dots on the Cutting Template indicate where it is helpful to maintain a ¼" seam allowance (Photo 5). When joining two pieces, match them at the dot end of the ¼" seam line; don't worry if the other end isn't even after stitching. If there aren't any dots, center one piece on the other to stitch.

## assemble blocks
**1** For one star block, use top piece from each stack. In each section (A, B, and C), join

pieces 1 and 2, matching ends of seams that have dots (Photo 6). Press seams toward each piece 1.

**2** Add piece 3 to each section and press seams toward each piece 3 (Photo 7).

**3** Before sewing together sections A and B, trim edges to straighten seam line (Photo 8). Join sections A and B, matching seams at bases of star points A1 and B1. Press seam in one direction.

**4** Before adding section C to AB unit, trim edges to straighten seam line. Sew together, centering star point C1 over A3 center so star legs look continuous (Photo 9). Press seam in one direction.

**5** Centering star, trim joined sections to 9½" square including seam allowances (Photo 10) to make a star block (Photo 11).

**6** Repeat steps 1–5 to make 13 star blocks total. Once familiar with "crazy" piecing, save time by chain-piecing all A1 and A2 pieces, then all B1 and B2 pieces, etc. Press, clip apart, and restack units before adding the next piece in the sequence.

## plan quilt layout and assemble sashing units

**From remaining portion of *each* assorted print fat quarter, cut:**

- 15—2½" squares (you will use 192 of the 195 total cut)

**1** Using a pencil, mark a diagonal line on wrong side of each assorted print 2½" square. (To prevent fabric from stretching as you draw the lines, place 220-grit sandpaper under squares.)

**2** Referring to **Quilt Assembly Diagram,** lay out star blocks in diagonal rows on a design wall or other large surface, leaving about 5" between rows and blocks. Between blocks and around block rows, lay out brown check 4½×9½" rectangles and 4½" squares. (Pieced sashing units are made with the same fabrics as adjacent star blocks. To match the look, you must lay out quilt center pieces prior to making sashing units.)

**3** Referring to **Quilt Assembly Diagram,** in corners of brown check A rectangles, position marked 2½" squares that match the background fabrics of adjacent star blocks (four 2½" squares on each rectangle).

**4** In corners of brown check A squares, position marked 2½" squares that match the background fabrics of adjacent star blocks (four 2½" squares on each square).

**5** Repeat Step 3 to position marked squares on brown check B rectangles, filling in corners not adjacent to a star block with assorted print squares. Repeat Step 4 to position marked squares on brown check B squares, filling in corners not adjacent to a star block with assorted print squares.

**6** Remove one brown check 4½×9½" rectangle and its 2½" squares from design wall. Referring to **Diagram 1** and noting placement of marked lines, align marked 2½" squares in opposite corners of rectangle. Stitch on marked lines, then trim excess fabric, leaving ¼" seam allowances. Press open attached triangles.

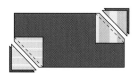

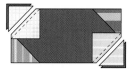

**DIAGRAM 1**

**7** In same manner, sew remaining marked 2½" squares in remaining corners of rectangle. Stitch, trim, and press as before to make a sashing rectangle. The sashing rectangle still should be 4½×9½" including seam allowances. Return sashing rectangle to design wall.

**8** Repeat steps 6 and 7 to make 36 sashing rectangles total.

**9** Referring to **Diagram 2** and steps 6 and 7, add marked 2½" squares to a brown check 4½" square to make a sashing square. The sashing square still should be 4½" square including seam allowances. Return sashing square to design wall. Repeat to make 12 sashing squares total.

**DIAGRAM 2**

## assemble quilt top

**1** Referring to **Quilt Assembly Diagram,** lay out small setting triangles at ends of each sashing diagonal row and large setting triangles at ends of each block diagonal row (except center block row).

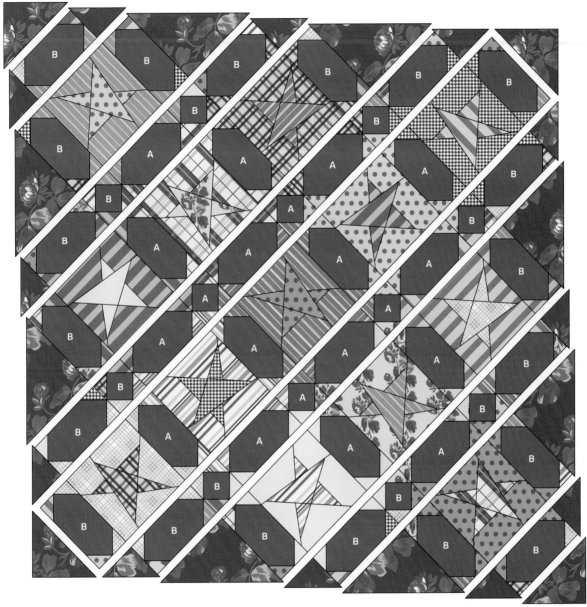

**QUILT ASSEMBLY DIAGRAM**

Sew together pieces in each row. Press seams away from sashing rectangles.

2 Join rows; press seams toward block rows. Add corner triangles to make quilt center. Press seams toward corner triangles. The quilt center should be 55⅝" square including seam allowances.

3 Cut and piece brown dot 4½×42" strips to make:
- 2—4½×63⅝" border strips
- 2—4½×55⅝" border strips

4 Sew short border strips to opposite edges of quilt center. Add long border strips to remaining edges to complete quilt top. Press all seams toward border.

"*As you make each cut, place stacked pieces in the corresponding area on the Cutting Template to help you stay organized.*"

—DESIGNERS JANET NESBITT AND PAM SOLIDAY

## finish quilt

1 Layer quilt top, batting, and backing; baste. (For details, see Complete Quilt, *page 175.*)

2 Quilt as desired. Karen Brown machine-outline-quilted each star ¼" from the edges, ending the stitching with a swirl in the center (**Quilting Diagram**). She quilted a freehand swirl pattern in the background of each block and in the sashing.

3 Bind with red tone-on-tone binding strips. (For details, see Complete Quilt.)

**QUILTING DIAGRAM**

## COLOR OPTION

To change the look of *Star Power*, quilt tester Laura Boehnke skipped the sashing and joined blocks in straight-set rows. Two ½"-wide finished borders visually separate the quilt center from a 4"-wide finished outer border.

# optical *illusion*

Don't be fooled. It may look like intricate piecing, but it's actually fast-and-easy appliqué on a classic Snowball block.

DESIGNER **ALLISON JANE SMITH OF PLAIDS AND PRINTS** (plaidsandprints.com)

## materials

- 20—18×22" pieces (fat quarters) *or* 4¼ yards total assorted prints and stripes in yellow, pink, blue, green, and brown (blocks, appliqués, border)
- ½ yard brown-and-pink print (binding)
- 3¼ yards backing fabric
- 58" square batting
- Lightweight fusible web
- Monofilament thread

**Finished quilt:** 49½" square
**Finished block:** 9" square

**Quantities** are for 44/45"-wide, 100% cotton fabrics. **Measurements** include ¼" seam allowances. Sew with right sides together unless otherwise stated.

## cut fabrics

Cut pieces in the following order.

To plan this quilt in your own colorway, use the **Coloring Diagram** on *Pattern Sheet 2.*

Patterns are on *Pattern Sheet 1.*

To use fusible web for appliquéing, complete the following steps.

**1** Lay fusible web paper side up over patterns. Use a pencil to trace each pattern the number of times indicated in cutting instructions, leaving ½" between tracings. Cut out fusible-web shapes roughly ¼" outside traced lines.

**2** Following manufacturer's instructions, press each fusible-web shape onto wrong side of designated fabric; let cool. Cut out fabric shapes on drawn lines; peel off paper backings.

**From assorted prints and stripes, cut:**

- 25—9½" squares
- 20—2½×9½" rectangles
- 100—2½" squares (25 sets of 4 matching squares for blocks)
- 40—2½" squares (20 sets of 2 matching squares for border units)
- 8—2½" squares for triangle-squares
- 25 of Pattern A
- 100 of Pattern B (25 sets of 4 pieces to match each Pattern A piece)
- 100 of Pattern C (25 sets of 4 matching pieces)

**From brown-and-pink print, cut:**

- 6—2½×42" binding strips

## assemble blocks

1  Use a pencil to mark a diagonal line on wrong side of each 2½" square. (To prevent fabric from stretching as you draw the lines, place 220-grit sandpaper under squares.)

2  Align a marked square with one corner of an assorted print or stripe 9½" square (Diagram 1; note direction of marked line). Sew on drawn line; trim excess fabric, leaving ¼" seam allowance. Press open attached triangle.

QUILT ASSEMBLY DIAGRAM

3  Repeat Step 2 to add three matching marked squares to remaining corners of 9½" square to make a Snowball block (Diagram 1; again note direction of drawn lines). The block should be 9½" square including seam allowances.

4  Repeat steps 2 and 3 to make 25 Snowball blocks total.

## appliqué blocks

1  Fold a Snowball block in half vertically and horizontally and finger-press. Then fold block in both directions diagonally and finger-press to create placement guidelines. (Fold lines will help you arrange appliqué shapes evenly.)

2  Referring to Appliqué Placement Diagram, lay out appliqué pieces on block; fuse in place following manufacturer's instructions. Using monofilament thread or threads that match the appliqués, straight-stitch or zigzag-stitch close to edges of each appliqué piece.

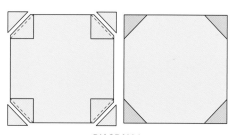

DIAGRAM 1

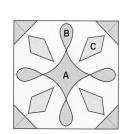

APPLIQUÉ PLACEMENT DIAGRAM

**3** Repeat steps 1 and 2 to appliqué 25 Snowball blocks total.

## assemble border units

**1** Align a marked 2½" square on one end of an assorted print or stripe 2½×9½" rectangle (Diagram 2; note direction of marked line). Sew on marked line; trim excess fabric, leaving ¼" seam allowance. Press open attached triangle. Add a matching marked square to opposite end of rectangle to make a border unit (Diagram 2; again note direction of marked line). The border unit should be 2½×9½" including seam

allowances. Repeat to make 20 border units total.

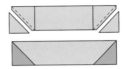

**DIAGRAM 2**

**2** Layer two remaining marked 2½" squares, aligning lines. Sew together on one marked line; trim excess fabric, leaving ¼" seam allowance (Diagram 3). Press unit open to make a triangle-square. The triangle-square should be 2½" square including seam allowances. Repeat to make four triangle-squares total.

**DIAGRAM 3**

## assemble quilt top

**1** Referring to Quilt Assembly Diagram, lay out blocks, border units, and triangle-squares in seven horizontal rows.

**2** Sew together pieces in each row. Press seams in one direction, alternating direction with each row.

**3** Join rows to complete quilt top. Press seams in one direction.

# COLOR OPTION

Make the easy-to-sew *Optical Illusion* even easier by eliminating the appliqués and cutting the corners for all the Snowball blocks from a single fabric. Warm-color prints—inspired by old-world, wood-block motifs and printed with natural dyes—give this cozy coverlet a soft, lived-in feeling when it's fresh from the machine.

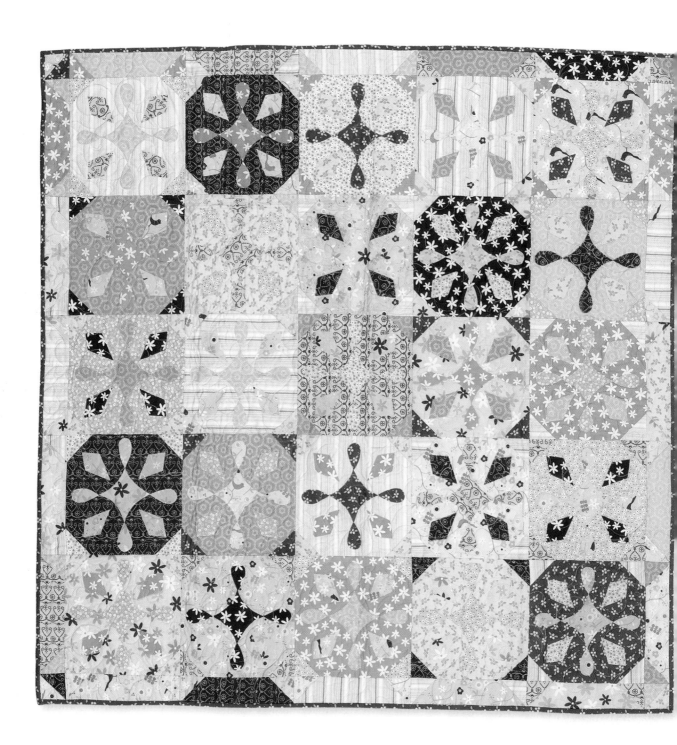

## finish quilt

1 Layer quilt top, batting, and backing; baste. (For details, see Complete Quilt, *page 175*.)

2 Quilt as desired. Designer Allison Jane Smith machine-quilted a swirl-and-leaf design across the quilt top.

3 Bind with brown and pink print binding strips. (For details, see Complete Quilt.)

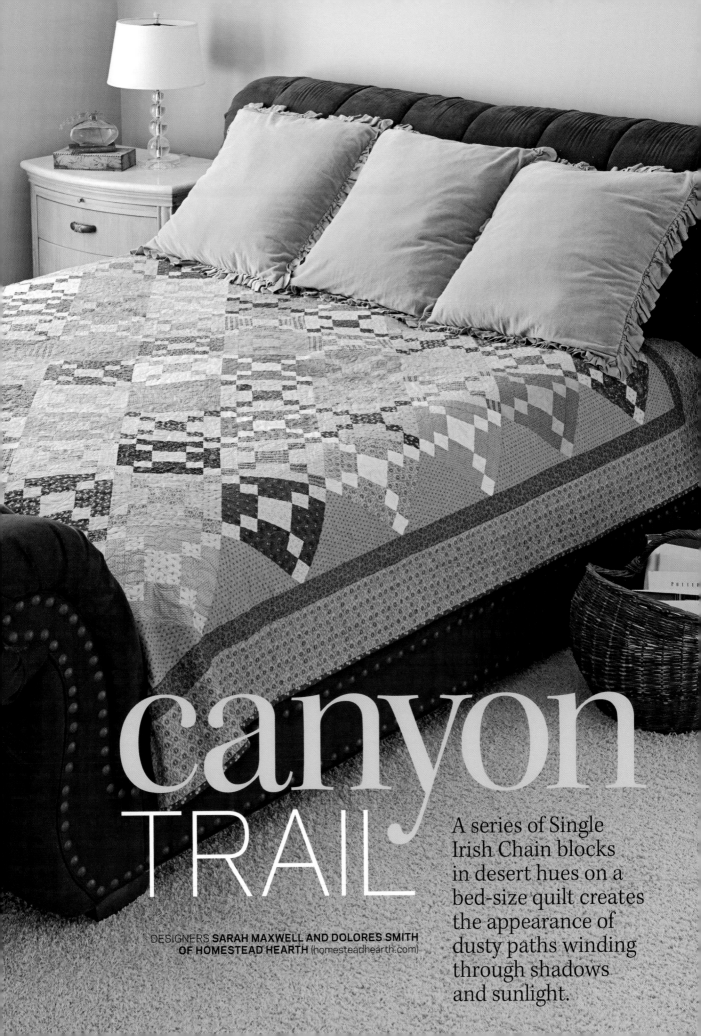

# canyon
## TRAIL

A series of Single Irish Chain blocks in desert hues on a bed-size quilt creates the appearance of dusty paths winding through shadows and sunlight.

DESIGNERS **SARAH MAXWELL AND DOLORES SMITH OF HOMESTEAD HEARTH** (homesteadhearth.com)

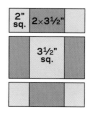

DIAGRAM 1

## materials

- 22—18×22" pieces (fat quarters) or 4⅜ yards total assorted medium to dark prints (blocks)
- 18—18×22" pieces (fat quarters) or 4 yards total assorted light prints and muslins (blocks)
- 1¼ yards gold print (setting and corner triangles)
- ⅔ yard brown print (inner border)
- 2⅛ yards light blue and tan print (outer border)
- ⅞ yard golden brown print (binding)
- 9⅓ yards backing fabric
- 112" square batting

Finished quilt: 103½" square (queen-size with 21" drop; king-size with 13" drop)
Finished block: 9" square

Optional sizes: Turn to *Pattern Sheet 2* for a chart of materials needed to make this quilt in other sizes.

Quantities are for 44/45"-wide, 100% cotton fabrics. Measurements include ¼" seam allowances. Sew with right sides together unless otherwise stated.

## cut fabrics

Cut pieces in the order that follows in each section.

**From gold print, cut:**
- 6—14" squares, cutting each diagonally twice in an X for 24 setting triangles total
- 2—7¼" squares, cutting each in half diagonally for 4 corner triangles total

**From brown print, cut:**
- 10—2×42" strips for inner border

**From light blue and tan print, cut:**
- 11—6×42" strips for outer border (Sarah and Dolores cut their outer border strips lengthwise so the stripe of the print runs parallel to the edges of the quilt. To do this, cut six 6×73" strips parallel to the selvages instead.)

**From golden brown print, cut:**
- 11—2½×42" binding strips

## cut and assemble dark blocks

The following instructions result in one dark block. Repeat cutting and assembly steps to make 49 dark blocks total.

**From one assorted medium or dark print, cut:**
- 4—2×6½" rectangles
- 4—2×3½" rectangles

**From one assorted light print or muslin, cut:**
- 1—3½" square
- 8—2" squares

1 Referring to **Diagram 1**, lay out four light print or muslin 2" squares, four medium or dark print 2×3½" rectangles, and the light print or muslin 3½" square in three rows.

2 Sew together pieces in each row. Press seams toward medium or dark print rectangles. Join rows to make a block center. Press seams away from center row.

3 Sew a light print or muslin 2" square to each end of a medium or dark print 2×6½" rectangle to make a pieced strip (**Diagram 2**). Press seam toward medium or dark print. Repeat to make a second pieced strip.

DIAGRAM 2

4 Add remaining medium or dark print 2×6½" rectangles to opposite edges of block center (**Diagram 3**). Press seams toward medium or dark print. Sew pieced strips to remaining edges of block center to make a dark block. Press seams toward block center. The block should be 9½" square including seam allowances.

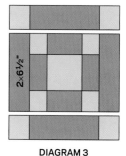

DIAGRAM 3

**SIZE OPTIONS:** For a chart of optional sizes, turn to *Pattern Sheet 2.*

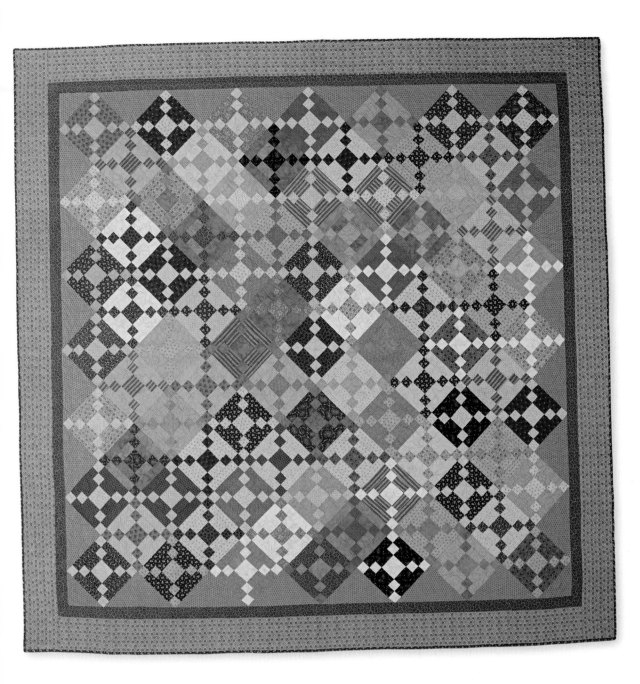

## cut and assemble light blocks

The following instructions result in one light block. Repeat cutting and assembly steps to make 36 light blocks total.

**From one light print or muslin, cut:**

- 4—2×6½" rectangles
- 4—2×3½" rectangles

**From one medium or dark print, cut:**

- 1—3½" square
- 8—2" squares

1 Referring to **Diagram 4**, lay out four medium or dark print 2" squares, four light print or muslin 2×3½" rectangles, and the medium or dark print 3½" square in three rows.

**DIAGRAM 4**

**2** Sew together pieces in each row. Press seams toward medium or dark print squares. Join rows to make a block center. Press seams toward center row.

**3** Sew a medium or dark print 2" square to each end of a light print or muslin 2×6½" rectangle to make a pieced strip (Diagram 5). Press seam toward medium or dark print. Repeat to make a second pieced strip.

**DIAGRAM 5**

**4** Add remaining light print or muslin 2×6½" rectangles to opposite edges of block center (Diagram 6). Press seams toward block center. Sew pieced strips to remaining edges of block center to make a light block. Press seams toward pieced strips. The block should be 9½" square including seam allowances.

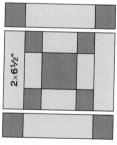

**DIAGRAM 6**

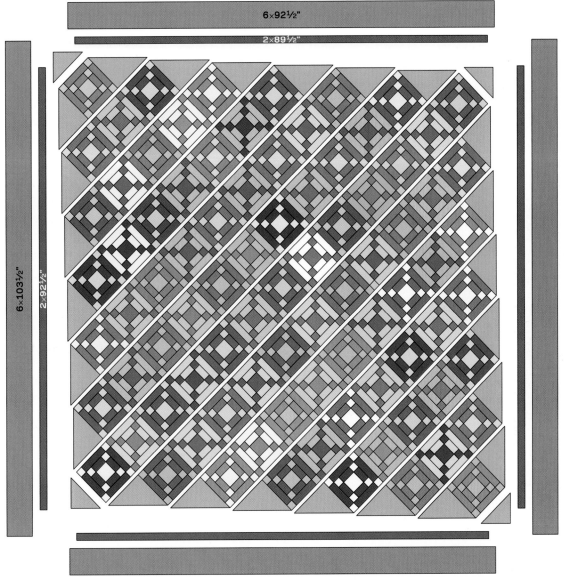

Diagram labels: 6×92½"  2×89½"  6×103½"  2×92½"

**QUILT ASSEMBLY DIAGRAM**

## assemble quilt center

1 Referring to **Quilt Assembly Diagram,** lay out blocks in 13 diagonal rows; alternate light and dark blocks, beginning and ending each row with a dark block. Place gold print setting triangles at ends of rows.

2 Sew together pieces in each row. Press seams toward dark blocks. Join rows; press seams in one direction.

3 Add gold print corner triangles to make quilt center. Press seams toward corner triangles. The quilt center should be 89½" square including seam allowances.

## add borders

**1** Cut and piece brown print
2×42" strips to make:
- 2—2×92½" inner border
  strips
- 2—2×89½" inner border
  strips

**2** Sew short inner border strips
to opposite edges of quilt
center. Add long inner border
strips to remaining edges.
Press all seams toward border.

**3** Cut and piece light blue and
tan print 6×42" strips to make:
- 2—6×103½" outer border
  strips
- 2—6×92½" outer border
  strips

**4** Sew short outer border strips
to opposite edges of quilt
center. Add long outer border
strips to remaining edges to
complete quilt top. Press all
seams toward outer border.

## finish quilt

**1** Layer quilt top, batting, and
backing; baste. (For details,
see Complete Quilt, *page 175*.)

**2** Quilt as desired. Connie
Gresham machine-quilted the
featured quilt with an allover
leaf-and-flower design
(**Quilting Diagram**).

**3** Bind with golden brown print
binding strips. (For details, see
Complete Quilt.)

QUILTING DIAGRAM

## COLOR OPTION

Quilt tester Laura Boehnke put a twist on a classic two-color combination by choosing blue and gray for her wall hanging version of *Canyon Trail*. Darks, mediums, and lights provide contrast.

Fussy-cutting an ikat print for the outer border gives the appearance of more intricate piecing without any additional work—perfect when you want to save time but not scrimp on style!

*To ease in a bit of extra fullness when the lengths of two units don't quite match, sew with the longer unit on the bottom.*

# it's a wrap

## about the method

Although designer Tari Colby used 6×6×¾" prestretched canvases as the foundations for this project, you can use any size prestretched canvas for your wall art. Simply adjust fabric requirements to allow at least 1½" on all sides of each prestretched canvas.

For a hard finish that's impervious to dust and moisture, Tari recommends brushing two coats of fabric decoupage medium onto the fabric surface.

## cut fabrics

Cut pieces in the following order.

**From *each* bright pink geometric, floral, and polka dot fat quarter, cut:**
- 3—9" squares

## assemble plaques

1 Place a bright pink geometric, floral, or polka dot 9" square right side down on a flat surface. Center a 6×6×¾" prestretched artist's canvas on fabric.

2 Wrap excess fabric to back side of prestretched canvas. Keeping fabric taut and smooth, staple excess to canvas frame beginning at center of each side edge.

3 Miter corners of fabric and secure with staples on back. Add sufficient staples to hold fabric straight and taut.

4 Following manufacturer's instructions, apply two coats of fabric decoupage medium, allowing finish to dry between coats. If desired, secure ribbon around edges with fabric glue to complete plaque.

5 Repeat steps 1–4 to make nine plaques total.

## materials

*for nine plaques*
- 18×22" rectangle (fat quarter) *each* of bright pink geometric, floral, and polka dot (squares)
- 9—6×6×¾" prestretched artist's canvases
- 6¾ yards ¾"-wide ribbon (optional)
- Staple gun and staples
- Fabric decoupage medium
- Fabric glue (optional)

**Finished plaque: 6×6×¾"**

**Quantities** are for 100% cotton fabrics.

## COLOR OPTION

When you're crazy about a fabric group and you can't bear to cut the lengths into small pieces, use big pieces to make striking wall art. This stunning assemblage features a series of black-and-white florals and prints, covering 12×36×¾", 12×16×¾", 9×12×¾", and 6×12×¾" prestretched canvases. For a colorful finish, consider trimming the side edges of each fabric-covered prestretched canvas with bright ¾"-wide grosgrain ribbon.

Don't buy them! Make your own exquisite wall plaques in gorgeous designer fabrics. It's easy and fun.

DESIGNER **TARI COLBY**

Whether precisely planned or stitched on the fly—you choose!—the simple strips of this elegant table runner provide an excellent introduction to sewing with silk.

# get
# IN LINE

DESIGNER **AMY WALSH OF BLUE UNDERGROUND STUDIOS**
(blueundergroundstudios.com)

## materials
- 11 to 15—9×22" pieces (fat eighths) assorted solid blue, green, and aqua dupioni silks (strips)
- ⅜ yard solid blue cotton (binding)
- 1½ yards cotton backing fabric
- 29×53" batting
- Lightweight fusible tricot interfacing (optional)

Finished table runner: 20½×44¼"

Quantities are for 44/45"-wide, 100% silk or 100% cotton fabrics.

Measurements include ¼" seam allowances. Sew with right sides together unless otherwise stated.

## cut fabrics
Cut pieces in the following order. If desired, fuse a sheer or ultralightweight interfacing to silk before cutting. Refer to "Silk Solutions," *page 52*, for more tips on cutting and sewing with silk.

**From each solid blue, green, and aqua silk, cut:**
- 4—1¾×21" strips

**From solid blue cotton, cut:**
- 4—2½×42" binding strips

## cut and assemble table runner top

Designer Amy Walsh used an improvisational method to construct her table runner. After cutting the silk fabrics into 21" lengths, she cut some in random shorter lengths. She pieced the shorter strips into rows at least 21" long. Amy experimented with the strip and row arrangement until the design was the size she desired.

If you prefer a more planned method for creating the pieced rows, set aside eight 1¾×21" strips and cut the rest of the 1¾×21" strips into the following lengths and amounts.

**From just-cut 1¾"-wide strips, cut:**

- 3—1¾×17" strips
- 4—1¾×15" strips
- 5—1¾×13½" strips
- 13—1¾×12½" strips
- 7—1¾×9½" strips
- 10—1¾×8½" strips
- 6—1¾×7½" strips
- 9—1¾×6½" strips
- 4—1¾×5" strips

**1** Referring to **Table Runner Assembly Diagram**, join an assorted solid 1¾×7½" strip and 1¾×15" strip to make a pieced row. Press seams open or in one direction. Amy presses all seams open so they are flatter and crisper.

**2** Referring to **Table Runner Assembly Diagram** for lengths of strips to use in each row, repeat Step 1 to make 27 pieced rows total.

**3** Working on a design wall, lay out eight 1¾×21" strips and the pieced rows, moving pieced rows left or right to ensure seams don't intersect

and strips in the same color aren't adjacent to one another.

**4** Join strips and rows to complete table runner top. Press seams open or in one direction. Referring to red

dotted lines on **Table Runner Assembly Diagram**, trim long edges of table runner to make a 20½×44¼" rectangle including seam allowances.

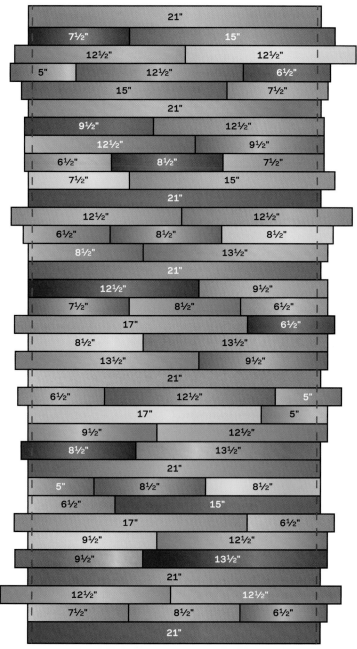

**TABLE RUNNER ASSEMBLY DIAGRAM**

# Silk Solutions

*Designer Amy Walsh offers these tips for working with silk.*

### PREVENTING FRAYING

- If you're concerned about fraying, fuse each fabric piece with a lightweight fusible tricot interfacing, such as Fusi-Knit from HTC, before cutting.
- Don't cut silk until you're ready to sew as shuffling increases fraying.
- Use a new rotary blade to ensure clean cuts.
- Resist the urge to pull loose threads.

### ASSEMBLING

- Pin with new, sharp pins.
- Replace your sewing machine needle with a new 80/12 sharps needle.
- Use cotton thread instead of polyester as there's less chance of cotton tearing or cutting the fabric at the seams.
- When sewing, hold fabric taut (but not stretched) in front of and behind the needle to prevent puckered seams.
- Press from the wrong side of the fabric with an iron on medium setting.
- Keep a lint roller near your ironing board to pick up threads that have frayed.

### FINISHING

- Select a low-loft batting so the silk does not appear puffy.
- Use a neutral thread that blends with your silk. Amy chose a dark gray quilting thread because black was used in the weave of the silk.

### CARING FOR

- Avoid laundering quilts made from dupioni silk. If it's necessary to clean a silk quilt, Amy recommends spot-washing or dry-cleaning.

## finish table runner

**1** Layer table runner top, batting, and backing; baste. (For details, see Complete Quilt, *page 175*.)

**2** Quilt as desired. Amy machine-quilted two or three straight lines in each row.

**3** Bind with solid blue binding strips. (For details, see Complete Quilt.)

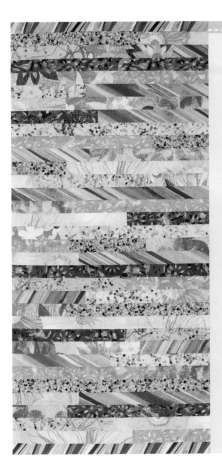

## COLOR OPTION

Punch up the pizzazz on a table runner by cutting its strips from bold, multicolor cotton prints, as quilt tester Laura Boehnke did. When the strips are pieced, a clear definition at the seam lines is less apparent than on the original table runner.

"By limiting the color palette to mostly pinks and yellows, the overall effect is more of impressionist art or a watercolor painting," Laura says. "This would also make a great wall hanging as an art piece."

*The backing can be made from a single fabric; however, it can be more elaborate if you wish. If you're up for the challenge, piece together leftover fabrics or fabrics in a different color scheme for a reversible table runner.*

Looks are deceiving. Though complex diagonal rows seem to appear, just two easy-to-sew blocks are straight-set side by side to make this stunning quilt.

# straight to the
# POINT

INSPIRED BY DESIGNER **ANNE MOSCICKI OF TOUCHWOOD QUILT DESIGN**

## materials
- 40— 18×22" pieces (fat quarters) assorted prints, stripes, and polka dots in pink, red, cream, tan, and brown (blocks, binding)
- 7½ yards backing fabric
- 90" square batting

**Finished quilt:** 81½" square
**Finished blocks:** 9" square

**Quantities** are for 44/45"-wide, 100% cotton fabrics. **Measurements** include ¼" seam allowances. Sew with right sides together unless otherwise stated.

## cut fabrics

Referring to the **Cutting Diagram**, cut pieces in the following order.

To plan this quilt in your own colorway, use the **Coloring Diagram** on *Pattern Sheet 2*.

**From assorted prints, stripes, and polka dots, cut:**

- 40—10¼" squares, cutting each diagonally twice in an X for 160 triangles total
- 369—3½" squares
- Enough 2½"-wide strips (from 19 of remaining fat quarters) to total 380" in length for binding

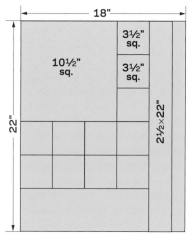

**CUTTING DIAGRAM**

**SIZE OPTIONS:** For a chart of optional sizes, turn to *Pattern Sheet 2.*

## assemble nine-patch blocks

Referring to **Diagram 1**, sew together nine assorted print, stripe, and polka dot 3½" squares in three horizontal rows. Press seams in one direction, alternating direction with each row. Join rows to make a Nine-Patch block. Press seams in one direction. The block should be 9½" square including seam allowances. Repeat to make 41 Nine-Patch blocks total.

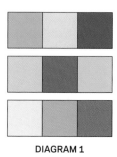

**DIAGRAM 1**

## assemble hourglass blocks

1 Sew together two assorted print, stripe, and polka dot triangles to make a triangle pair (**Diagram 2**). Press seam toward darker triangle. Repeat to make 80 triangle pairs total.

**DIAGRAM 2**

2 Join two triangle pairs to make an Hourglass block (**Diagram 3**). Press seam in one direction. The block should be 9½" square including seam allowances. Repeat to make 40 Hourglass blocks total.

**DIAGRAM 3**

## assemble quilt top

1 Referring to **Quilt Assembly Diagram**, lay out blocks in nine Horizontal rows, alternating Nine-Patch blocks and Hourglass blocks.

2 Sew together blocks in each row. Press seams toward Hourglass blocks.

3 Join rows to complete quilt top. Press seams in one direction.

QUILT ASSEMBLY DIAGRAM

## finish quilt

1  Layer quilt top, batting, and backing; baste. (For details, see Complete Quilt, *page 175.*)

2  Quilt as desired. Machine-quilter Nancy Sharr stitched an allover leaf-and-vine design across the quilt top.

3  Using diagonal seams, join assorted print, stripe, and polka dot 2½"-wide strips to make a pieced binding strip. Bind quilt with pieced binding strip. (For details, see Complete Quilt.)

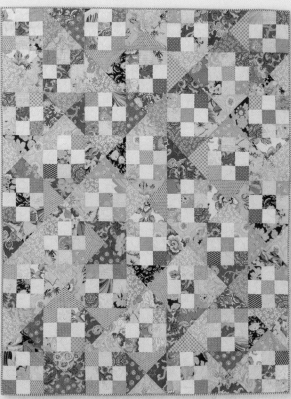

# COLOR OPTION

If modern is more your style, choose a mix of contemporary fabrics in green, turquoise, and brown hues to make your own version of *Straight to the Point*. Editor Jennifer Keltner selected a mix of florals, contemporary prints, and polka dots, then used an unregimented placement of lights and darks to make this knockout quilt, *above left*.

If you prefer a lighter look, select an assortment of florals and complementary small-scale prints in pastels and lighter colors to make a version similar to designer Anne Moscicki's quilt, *above right*. To mimic this stash-busting quilt, choose a favorite multicolor print and pull colors from it. Avoid the temptation to match the fabrics; just use a merry mix of colors and prints. Anne used nearly a dozen green fabrics, from pale green and chartreuse to acid green and forest. Squares of bright blue sprinkled across the quilt top create an unexpected pop.

Get a jump on the season. Start and finish this simple table runner before fall's spectacular color show begins.

# autumn *breeze*

DESIGNER **DARLENE ZIMMERMAN OF NEEDLINGS** (feedsacklady.com)

## materials

- 6—9×22" pieces (fat eighths) assorted light prints in cream and tan (blocks, setting triangles)
- 6—4½×22" pieces assorted dark prints in green, brown, gold, and rust (blocks)
- ¾ yard multicolor leaf print (border, binding)
- 1½ yards backing fabric
- 25×54" batting
- 1¾ yards ³⁄₁₆"-wide rickrack: black

Finished table runner: 20×48¾"
Finished blocks: 3" square

Quantities are for 44/45"-wide, 100% cotton fabrics. Measurements include ¼" seam allowances. Sew with right sides together unless otherwise stated.

## cut fabrics

Cut pieces in the following order.

To speed the cutting process, designer Darlene Zimmerman prefers to use the Easy Angle and Companion Angle acrylic template tools from Simplicity. If you're using those tools, refer to "Quick Cuts," *page 62,* for cutting instructions for the light and dark prints.

**From each light print, cut:**

- 4—4¼" squares, cutting each diagonally twice in an X for 16 large triangles total (you will use 88 of the 96 triangles cut)
- 8—1⅞" squares, cutting each in half diagonally for 16 small triangles total
- 8—1½" squares

**From each dark print, cut:**
- 8—1⅞" squares, cutting each in half diagonally for 16 small triangles total
- 12—1½" squares

**From multicolor leaf print, cut:**
- 3—2½×42" binding strips
- 2—4×27" border strips
- 2—4×19" border strips
- 2—4×15" border strips

**From rickrack, cut:**
- 24—2½"-long pieces

## assemble leaf blocks

1 For a set of four blocks, gather all small triangles and 1½" squares from one light print and one dark print.

2 Position a 2½"-long rickrack piece diagonally on right side of a light print 1½" square **(Diagram 1)**. Topstitch in place to make a stem unit. Repeat to make four stem units total.

**DIAGRAM 1**

3 Sew together a light print small triangle and a dark print small triangle to make a triangle-square **(Diagram 2)**. Press seam toward dark print. Repeat to make 16 triangle-squares total.

**DIAGRAM 2**

4 Referring to **Diagram 3**, sew together four triangle-squares, one light print 1½" square, three dark print 1½" squares, and one stem unit in three rows. Press seams as shown in diagram. Join rows to make a leaf block; press seams toward middle row. The leaf block should be 3½" square including seam allowances. Repeat to make four matching leaf blocks total.

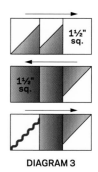

**DIAGRAM 3**

5 Repeat steps 1–4 to make 24 leaf blocks total (four from each color combination); you will use 23.

## assemble hourglass blocks and setting triangles

1 Join two assorted light print large triangles to make a setting triangle **(Diagram 4)**. Press seam toward right-hand triangle. Repeat to make 44 setting triangles total. Put aside 12 setting triangles to be used as side setting triangles in the table runner top.

# Quick Cuts

To shorten the time it takes to cut the pieces for this project, designer Darlene Zimmerman used the Easy Angle and Companion Angle acrylic tools from Simplicity (*simplicity.com*). If you're using those tools, follow these cutting instructions. For more details, refer to the instructions that come with the templates.

**From *each* light print, cut:**
- 2—2×21" strips, cutting them into 15 Companion Angle triangles*
- 1—1½×21" strip, cutting it into 16 Easy Angle triangles**
- 8—1½" squares

**From *each* dark print, cut:**
- 1—1½×21" strip, cutting it into 16 Easy Angle triangles**
- 12—1½" squares

*If you want to chain-piece the resulting large triangles, layer strips of two different light prints right sides together and cut with the Companion Angle tool.

**If you want to chain-piece the resulting small triangles, layer light and dark print strips right sides together and cut with the Easy Angle tool.

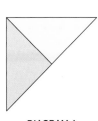

**DIAGRAM 4**

**2** Join two remaining setting triangles to make an hourglass block **(Diagram 5)**. Press seam in one direction. The hourglass block should be 3½" square including seam allowances. Repeat to make 16 hourglass blocks total.

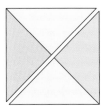

**DIAGRAM 5**

*Rickrack stems save time!*

## assemble table runner top

1 Alternating blocks, lay out 23 leaf blocks, all the hourglass blocks, and the 12 side setting triangles in nine diagonal rows (Table Runner Assembly Diagram). Sew together pieces in each row. Press seams toward hourglass blocks and side setting triangles.

2 Join rows to make table runner center. Press seams in one direction.

3 Center multicolor leaf print 4×27" border strips on long edges of table runner center; sew strips to edges. Press seams toward border. Trim edges of border strips even with angled edges of table runner center (Diagram 6).

4 Sew multicolor leaf print 4×15" border strips to opposite short edges of table runner center. Press strips open, pressing seams toward border. Trim strips even with edges of adjacent border strips (Diagram 7). Add multicolor leaf print 4×19" border strips to remaining edges of quilt center. Press and trim as before to complete table runner top (Diagram 8).

## finish table runner

1 Layer table runner top, batting, and backing; baste. (For details, see Complete Quilt, *page 175*.)

**TABLE RUNNER ASSEMBLY DIAGRAM**

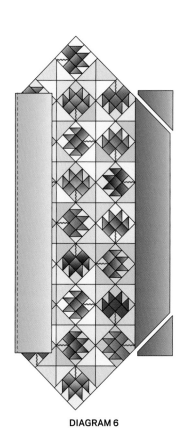

**DIAGRAM 6**

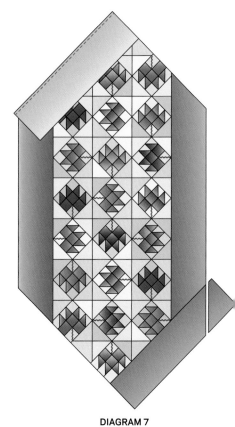

**DIAGRAM 7**

**2** Quilt as desired. Darlene hand-quilted a row of stitches vertically through each dark print square in the leaf blocks. She stipple-quilted the light print areas of the table runner center. In the border she highlighted the leaf motifs of the print with free-motion stitching.

**3** Bind with multicolor leaf print binding strips. (For details, see Complete Quilt.)

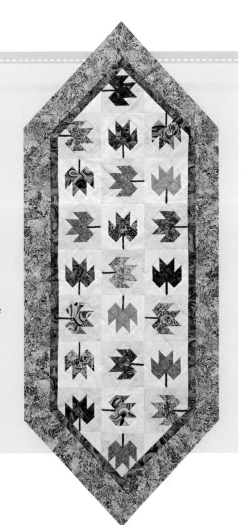

## COLOR OPTION

An added inner border (cut 1¼" wide) repeats the color of the light blue backgrounds in the leaf blocks. To make blocks that appear to be straight set, quilt tester Laura Boehnke alternated two background fabrics in the leaf blocks, then pieced the same fabrics into hourglass units and side setting triangles. For stems, Laura backed a green print with no-sew fusible web, then rotary-cut it into strips with a pinking blade.

DIAGRAM 8

··· tip ···

*If sewing tiny triangle-squares seems challenging, consider making them larger than necessary, then trimming them to the correct size.*

DESIGNERS (BAG) **JOANNA FIGUEROA OF FIG TREE & CO.** (figtreequilts.com), (PILLOW) **CAMILLE ROSKELLEY OF THIMBLE BLOSSOMS** (thimbleblossoms.com), and (TABLE MAT) **JO MORTON OF JO MORTON QUILTS** (jomortonquilts.com)

# pick six

Four darks and three lights give you the option to make any of these three fat-quarter friendly projects. (Save the extra for your stash!)

## materials *for the bag*

- 3—18×22" pieces (fat quarters) assorted cream-and-red prints (bag sides, lining)
- 3—18×22" pieces (fat quarters) assorted red prints (bag bottom, lining, flap, strap)
- 1½ yards iron-on fusible polyester fleece
- 1"-diameter button: cream
- Magnetic snap closure

Finished bag: 11×12¾×3"

Quantities are for 100% cotton fabrics.
Measurements include ¼" seam allowances. Sew with right sides together unless otherwise stated.

**From each of two cream-and-red prints, cut:**
- 1—7¾×14½" rectangle
- 4—2½×11" strips

**From third cream-and-red print, cut:**
- 1—7¾×14½" rectangle
- 6—2½×11" strips

**From red print No. 1, cut:**
- 1—8×14½" rectangle
- 2 of Bag Flap Pattern

**From red print No. 2, cut:**
- 2—6×18" strips

**From red print No. 3, cut:**
- 1—7¾×14½" rectangle

**From fusible fleece, cut:**
- 1—14½×29" rectangle
- 1 of Bag Flap Pattern
- 1—1½×34½" strip

## cut fabrics

Cut pieces in the following order. **Bag Flap Pattern** is on *Pattern Sheet 1.* To make a template for the bag flap, trace pattern onto a large sheet of paper and cut out on drawn solid outer lines; transfer markings.

**3** Following manufacturer's instructions, fuse 14½×29" fleece rectangle to wrong side of outer bag unit. Designer Joanna Figueroa quilted the outer bag unit by stitching-in-the-ditch between the cream and red print strips and by topstitching the red print rectangle about ⅛" from seams.

**4** Following manufacturer's instructions, attach female portion of magnetic snap closure to right side of outer bag unit, centering it 7¼" from side edge and about 4½" from top edge (Diagram 3).

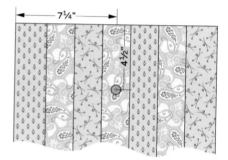

7¼"

4½"

**DIAGRAM 3**

**5** With right sides together, fold outer bag unit in half to make a 14½" square. Sew side edges of outer bag (Diagram 4). Press seam open.

## assemble and quilt bag body

**1** Lay out seven assorted cream-and-red print 2½×11" strips in a row (Diagram 1). Sew together strips to make a 14½×11" pieced rectangle. Press seams in one direction. Repeat with remaining assorted cream and red print 2½×11" strips to make a second 14½×11" pieced rectangle.

make a 14½×29" outer bag unit (Diagram 2). Press seams toward red print rectangle.

14½×8"

**DIAGRAM 2**

2½×11"

**DIAGRAM 1**

**2** With right sides together, sew a 14½×11" pieced rectangle to each long edge of red print No. 1—14½×8" rectangle to

**DIAGRAM 4**

**6** To shape a flat bottom on outer bag, refer to **Diagram 5** and at one corner match center bottom of bag to side seam line, creating a flattened triangle. Measure and mark on seam allowance 1½" from point of triangle. Draw a 3"-long line across the triangle, and sew on drawn line. Trim excess fabric, leaving ¼" seam allowance. Repeat at remaining bottom corner to make bag body. Turn bag body to right side.

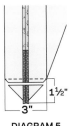

**DIAGRAM 5**

## assemble bag lining

**1** Referring to **Diagram 6**, lay out three cream and red print 7¾×14½" rectangles and red print No. 3—7¾×14½" rectangle in a row. Sew together rectangles to make bag lining, leaving a 5" opening between center rectangles. Trim bag lining to 14½×29" including seam allowances.

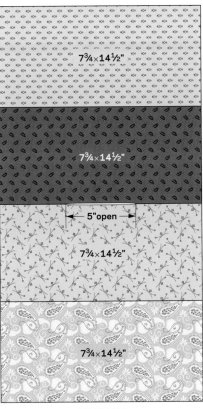

7¾×14½"

7¾×14½"

5"open

7¾×14½"

7¾×14½"

**DIAGRAM 6**

**2** Fold bag lining in half; sew together side edges as in Assemble and Quilt Bag Body, Step 5.

**3** Shape a flat bottom for lining as in Assemble and Quilt Bag Body, Step 6. Leave lining wrong side out.

## assemble flap

**1** Fuse fleece bag flap piece to wrong side of one red print No. 1 bag flap piece.

**2** Referring to Bag Flap Pattern for placement and following manufacturer's instructions, attach male portion of magnetic snap closure to right side of fused flap piece.

**3** Referring to **Diagram 7**, sew together fused flap piece and remaining red print No. 1 flap piece, leaving top edge open. Trim seam allowance and clip curves; turn to right side. Topstitch ⅛" from curved edge to make flap.

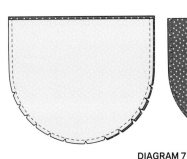

**DIAGRAM 7**

> **"**Creating a lined bag from six fat quarters is sheer magic. It's amazing what can be done with small bits of fabric.**"**
> —JOANNA FIGUEROA

## assemble bag

**1** With magnetic closure facing away from bag body, center straight edge of bag flap along upper back edge of bag body; baste (**Diagram 8**).

**DIAGRAM 8**

**2** Referring to **Diagram 9**, slip bag body inside lining, matching side seams; pin. (The flap is sandwiched between bag body and lining.) Sew upper edges together.

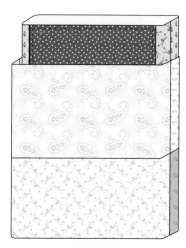

**DIAGRAM 9**

**3** Turn bag right side out through opening in lining bottom. Slip-stitch opening closed. Insert lining into bag. Press upper edges of bag. Topstitch ¼" from upper edge through all layers.

## assemble and attach strap

**1** Join red print No. 2—6×18" strips to make a 6×35½" strap piece.

**2** Fold short ends of strap piece under ½", wrong side inside; press (**Diagram 10**).

**DIAGRAM 10**

**3** Referring to **Diagram 11**, fold strap piece in half, wrong side inside. Press, then unfold. Fold long edges to meet in center; press again.

**DIAGRAM 11**

**4** Referring to **Diagram 12**, open one long edge of strap piece and center 1½×34½" fleece strip inside along fold line; fuse. Refold long edge toward center of strip. Fold in half lengthwise, matching folded edges, and press. Topstitch along all edges to make strap.

**DIAGRAM 12**

**5** Align one end of strap, centered at bag side, 1½" below top edge. Stitch securely in place (**Diagram 13**). Repeat with remaining end of strap at opposite bag side.

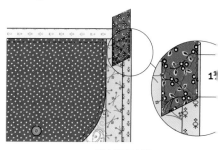

**DIAGRAM 13**

**6** Sew button to flap front to complete bag.

**3** Align a marked cream and red print square with opposite corners of a red print 3" square (**Diagram 1**; note direction of drawn lines). Sew on drawn lines, then trim excess, leaving ¼" seam allowances. Press open attached triangles, pressing seams toward triangles.

DIAGRAM 1

**4** In same manner, add a third marked cream and red print square to one remaining corner, again noting direction of drawn line (**Diagram 2**). Stitch, trim, and press as before to make a unit. The unit should be 3" square including seam allowances.

DIAGRAM 2

**5** Repeat steps 3 and 4 to make four units total.

**6** Sew together four matching units in pairs (**Diagram 3**). Press seams in opposite directions. Join pairs to make a block. Press seam in one direction. The block should be 5½" square including seam allowances.

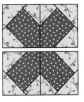

DIAGRAM 3

## materials *for the pillow*

- 2—18×22" pieces (fat quarters) assorted cream and red prints (blocks, border)
- 4—18×22" pieces (fat quarters) assorted red prints (blocks, pillow back)
- ½ yard muslin (pillow form)
- 20×15" piece iron-on fusible polyester fleece or batting
- Polyester fiberfill (pillow form)

Finished block: 5" square
Finished pillow: 19×14"

Quantities are for 100% cotton fabrics.
Measurements include ¼" seam allowances. Sew with right sides together unless otherwise stated.

## cut fabrics

Cut pieces in the following order.

**From one cream-and-red print, cut:**
- 72—1¾" squares

**From remaining cream and red print, cut:**
- 2—2¾×20" border strips
- 2—2¾×10½" border strips

**From red print No. 1, cut:**
- 1—5½×12" rectangle
- 8—3" squares

**From red print No. 2, cut:**
- 1—5½×12" rectangle
- 8—3" squares

**From red print No. 3, cut:**
- 1—5×12" rectangle
- 8—3" squares

**From red print No. 4, cut:**
- 1—15×16" rectangle

**From muslin, cut:**
- 2—15×20" rectangles

## assemble blocks

**1** Use a pencil to mark a diagonal line on wrong side of each cream and red print 1¾" square. (To prevent fabric from stretching as you draw lines, place 220-grit sandpaper under each square.)

**2** For one block you will need 12 cream and red print 1¾" marked squares and four matching red print 3" squares.

**7** Repeat steps 2–6 to make six blocks total (two matching blocks from each of three red prints).

## assemble and quilt pillow top

**1** Referring to **Pillow Top Assembly Diagram**, lay out blocks in two horizontal rows. Join pieces in each row. Press seams in opposite directions.

**2** Join rows to make pillow center. Press seam in one direction. The pillow center should be 15½×10½" including seam allowances.

**3** Sew cream and red print 2¾×10½" border strips to short edges of pillow center. Join cream and red print 2¾×20" border strips to remaining edges to make pillow top. Press all seams toward border. The pillow top should be 20×15" including seam allowances.

**4** Center and fuse 20×15" fleece or batting rectangle to wrong side of pillow top. Quilt as desired. Designer Camille Roskelley stitched vertical lines ½" apart across the pillow top.

## make pillow form

Layer two muslin 15×20" rectangles together; join with ½" seam, leaving a 5" opening along one long edge for stuffing. Turn right side out; press. Stuff to desired firmness with polyester fiberfill. Slip-stitch opening closed to make 19×14" pillow form.

## finish pillow

**1** Lay out red print No. 1 and No. 2—5½×12" rectangles and red print No. 3—5×12" rectangle in a row **(Diagram 4)**. Join pieces to make a 15×12" small back unit; press seams in one direction.

**2** Turn under 1" along one 15" edge of small back unit; press. Turn under 1" again and stitch in place to hem small back unit.

**3** In same manner, turn under one 15" edge of red print No. 4—15×16" rectangle twice; hem to make large back unit.

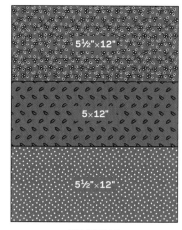

**DIAGRAM 4**

**4** Referring to **Diagram 5**, overlap hemmed edges of small and large back units by about 4" to make a 20×15" pillow back. Baste overlapped edges.

**5** Layer pillow top and pillow back with right sides together; join with ½" seam. Turn right side out. Insert pillow form through opening to complete pillow.

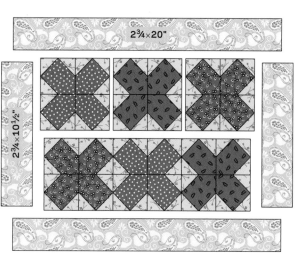

**PILLOW TOP ASSEMBLY DIAGRAM**

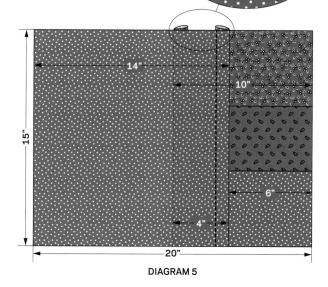

**DIAGRAM 5**

## materials *for the table mat*
- 2—18×22" pieces (fat quarters) assorted cream-and-red prints (blocks, border, backing)
- 4—18×22" pieces (fat quarters) assorted red prints (blocks, border, backing, binding)
- 26½×21" batting

Finished table mat: 23½×16½"
Finished block: 3½" square

Quantities are for 100% cotton fabrics.
Measurements include ¼" seam allowances. Sew with right sides together unless otherwise stated.

## cut fabrics
Cut pieces in the following order.
  Designer Jo Morton used a single-fold binding of 1⅛"-wide strips. If you wish to use a double-fold binding, cut your binding strips 2½" wide.

**From *each* assorted cream print, refer to Cutting Diagram 1, *page 74*, and cut:**
- 1—8×21" rectangle for backing
- 6—4¾" squares
- 5—1½×4" rectangles
- 1—2" square

**From *each* of two red prints, cut:**
- 4—4¾" squares
- 3—1½×4" rectangles
- 1—2" square

**From a third red print, refer to Cutting Diagram 2, *page 74*, and cut:**
- 1—11½×21" rectangle for backing
- 4—4¾" squares
- 4—1½×4" rectangles

**From a fourth red print, cut:**
- 5—1⅛×21" binding strips

## assemble hourglass blocks
1 Use a pencil to mark a diagonal line on wrong side of each cream print 4¾" square. (To prevent fabric from stretching as you draw lines, place 220-grit sandpaper under each square.)

2 Layer a marked cream print square atop an assorted red print 4¾" square. Sew together with two seams, stitching ¼" on each side of drawn line (Diagram 1). Cut apart on drawn line to make two triangle units. Press each triangle unit open, pressing seams toward red print, to make two large triangle-squares. Each should be 4⅜" square including seam allowances.

**DIAGRAM 1**

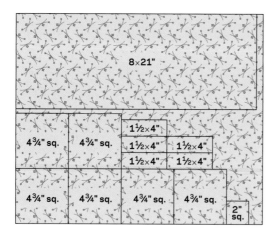

CUTTING DIAGRAM 1

In the cutting diagram 1: 8×21", 4¾" sq., 4¾" sq., 1½×4", 1½×4", 1½×4", 1½×4", 1½×4", 4¾" sq., 4¾" sq., 4¾" sq., 4¾" sq., 2" sq.

CUTTING DIAGRAM 2

In cutting diagram 2: 11½×21", 1½×4", 1½×4", 1½×4", 1½×4", 4¾" sq., 4¾" sq., 4¾" sq., 4¾" sq.

**3** Mark a diagonal line perpendicular to seam line on wrong side of one large triangle-square.

**4** Referring to **Diagram 2**, layer marked large triangle-square atop unmarked large triangle-square, with each red print triangle facing a cream print triangle. Sew together with two seams, stitching ¼" on each side of drawn line. Cut apart on drawn line to make two triangle units. Press each unit open to make two matching Hourglass blocks. Each block should be 4" square including seam allowances.

DIAGRAM 2

**5** Repeat steps 2–4 to make 24 Hourglass blocks total.

**6** Referring to **Diagram 3**, to reduce bulk clip ¼" into seam allowances of Hourglass blocks up to seam lines on each side of seam intersections. (Clips will be ½" apart.) Press block seam allowances toward red print triangles. Press clipped intersections open to create tiny Four-Patches on wrong side of blocks.

DIAGRAM 3

## assemble table mat center

Referring to **Table Mat Assembly Diagram**, lay out Hourglass blocks in four horizontal rows, alternating positions of red and cream prints. Sew together blocks in each row. Press seams open. Join rows to make table mat center; press seams open. The table mat center should be 21½×14½" including seam allowances.

## assemble and add border

**1** Use a pencil to mark a diagonal line on wrong side of each cream print 2" square.

**2** Using marked cream print squares and unmarked red print 2" squares, repeat Assemble Hourglass Blocks, Step 2, to make four small triangle-squares. Trim each small triangle-square to 1½" square including seam allowances.

**3** Referring to **Table Mat Assembly Diagram**, sew together three cream print 1½×4" rectangles and three red print 1½×4" rectangles to make a long border strip. Press seams open. The strip should be 1½×21½" including seam allowances. Repeat to make a second long border strip.

**4** Sew together two small triangle-squares, two cream print 1½×4" rectangles, and two red print 1½×4" rectangles to make a short border strip (**Table Mat Assembly Diagram**; note rotation of small triangle-squares). Press seams open.

**TABLE MAT ASSEMBLY DIAGRAM**

**2** Layer table mat top, batting, and backing rectangle; baste. Quilt as desired. Jo stitched in the ditch of the diagonal Hourglass block seams.

**3** Bind with red print binding strips using the following single-fold method. With the wrong side inside, fold under 1" at one end of the binding strip; press. Turn under and press a ¼" seam allowance on one long edge of the strip before joining the other long edge to the quilt. This pressed edge will be hand-stitched to the back of the quilt after the binding strip is sewn to the quilt top.

The strip should be 1½×16½" including seam allowances. Repeat to make a second short border strip.

**5** Referring to **Table Mat Assembly Diagram** for positions of red and cream print rectangles, sew long border strips to long edges of table mat center. Add short border strips to remaining edges to complete table mat top. Press all seams toward border.

## finish table mat

**1** Referring to **Diagram 4**, sew together cream print 8×21" rectangles and red print 11½×21" rectangle to make a backing rectangle. Press seams toward red print rectangle. The backing rectangle should be 26½×21" including seam allowances.

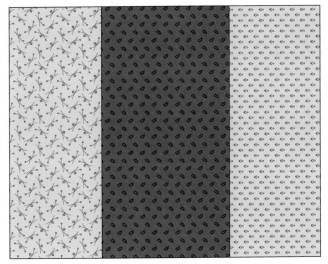

**DIAGRAM 4**

strips

Contrasting colors and values showcase a dynamic design that is simplified with strip piecing.

DESIGNER **EMILY HERRICK OF CRAZY OLD LADIES**
(crazyoldladiesquilts.blogspot.com)

# b.y.o.p.
*build your own plaid*

## materials

- 6—2½×42" precut strips *or* ½ yard total assorted brown prints (blocks, border No. 1)
- 8—2½×42" precut strips *or* ⅝ yard total assorted tan prints (blocks, border No. 1)
- 12—2½×42" precut strips *or* 1 yard total assorted cream prints (blocks, border No. 1)
- 11—2½×42" precut strips *or* 1 yard total assorted blue prints (blocks, border No. 3)
- 1 yard brown check (border No. 4)
- ⅝ yard mottled red (binding)
- 12—2½×42" precut strips *or* 1 yard total assorted red prints (sashing, border No. 2)
- 4 yards backing fabric
- 71" square batting

Finished quilt: 62½" square
Finished block: 18" square

**Quantities** are for precut 2½×42" strips and 44/45"-wide, 100% cotton fabrics.
**Measurements** include ¼" seam allowances. Sew with right sides together unless otherwise stated.

## cut fabrics

Cut pieces in the following order.

To plan this quilt in your own colorway, use the Coloring Diagram on *Pattern Sheet 2.*

**From assorted brown prints, cut:**
- 6—2½×31" strips

**From assorted tan prints, cut:**
- 8—2½×31" strips

**From assorted cream prints, cut:**
- 10—2½×31" strips
- 8—2½×6½" rectangles
- 4—2½×4½" rectangles
- 16—2½" squares

**From *five* assorted blue print strips, cut:**
- 8—2½×14½" rectangles
- 8—2½×10½" rectangles

**From brown check, cut:**
- 6—4½×42" strips for border No. 4

**From mottled red, cut:**
- 7—2½×42" binding strips

## assemble block centers

**1** Referring to **Diagram 1**, sew together three assorted brown print 2½×31" strips and two assorted tan print 2½×31" strips to make strip set A. Press seams toward tan print strips. Cut strip set into 12—2½"-wide A segments.

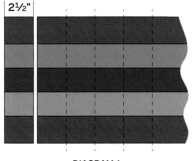

2½"

**DIAGRAM 1**

**2** Referring to **Diagram 2**, sew together three assorted tan print 2½×31" strips and two assorted cream print 2½×31" strips to make strip set B. Press seams toward tan print strips. Cut strip set into eight 2½"-wide B segments.

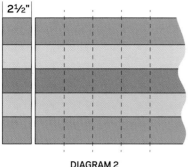

2½"

**DIAGRAM 2**

**3** Join three A segments and two B segments to make a block center (**Diagram 3**). Press seams in one direction. The block center should be 10½" square including seam allowances. Repeat to make four block centers total.

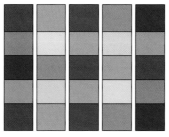

**DIAGRAM 3**

## assemble blocks

**1** Sew assorted blue print 2½×10½" rectangles to opposite edges of a block center (**Diagram 4**). Join assorted blue print 2½×14½" rectangles to remaining edges to make a framed block center. Press all seams toward blue print rectangles. The framed block center should be 14½" square including seam allowances. Repeat to make four framed block centers total.

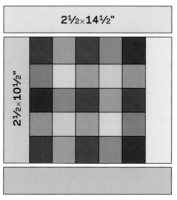

2½×14½"

2½×10½"

**DIAGRAM 4**

**2** Referring to **Diagram 5**, sew together four assorted cream print 2½×31" strips and three assorted tan or brown print 2½×31" strips to make strip set C. Press seams toward tan or brown print strips. Repeat to make a second strip set C. Cut strip sets into 24—2½"-wide C segments.

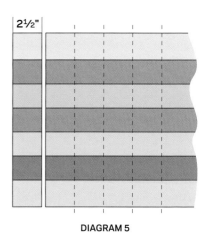

2½"

**DIAGRAM 5**

**3** Sew C segments to opposite edges of a framed block center (**Diagram 6**). Press seams toward blue print rectangles.

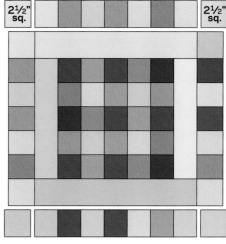

2½" sq.      2½" sq.

**DIAGRAM 6**

**4** Add an assorted cream print 2½" square to each end of two C segments to make two long C segments (**Diagram 6**). Press seams toward cream print squares. Join long C segments to remaining edges of framed block center to make a block. Press seams toward blue print rectangles. The block should be 18½" square including seam allowances.

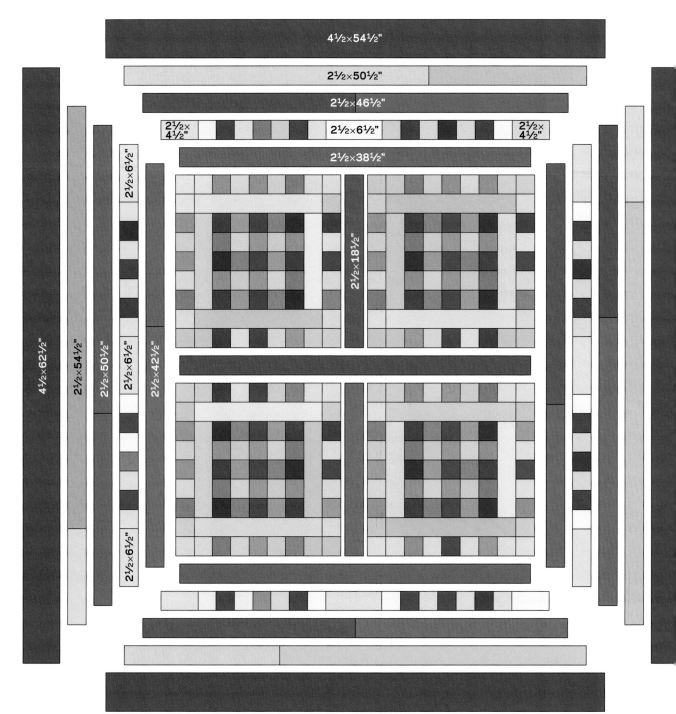

QUILT ASSEMBLY DIAGRAM

**5** Repeat steps 3 and 4 to make four blocks total. Set aside remaining C segments for border No. 1.

## assemble quilt center

**1** Cut and piece assorted red print 2½×42" strips to make:
- 2—2½×42½" sashing strips
- 3—2½×38½" sashing strips
- 2—2½×18½" sashing strips

**2** Referring to **Quilt Assembly Diagram**, sew together two blocks and one 2½×18½" sashing strip to make a block row. Press seams toward sashing. Repeat to make a second block row.

**3** Join block rows and 2½×38½" sashing strips. Add 2½×42½" sashing strips to remaining edges to make quilt center. Press all seams toward sashing. The quilt center should be 42½" square including seam allowances.

## assemble and add border No. 1

**1** Referring to **Quilt Assembly Diagram**, sew together two assorted cream print 2½×4½" rectangles, two C segments, and one assorted cream print 2½×6½" rectangle to make a short border No. 1 strip. Press seams toward cream print rectangles. The strip should be 2½×42½" including seam allowances. Repeat to make a second short border No. 1 strip.

**2** Referring to **Quilt Assembly Diagram**, sew together three assorted cream print 2½×6½" rectangles and two C segments to make a long border No. 1 strip. Press seams toward cream print rectangles. The strip should be 2½×46½" including seam allowances. Repeat to make a second long border No. 1 strip.

**3** Join short border No. 1 strips to opposite edges of quilt center. Add long border No. 1 strips to remaining edges. Press seams toward border No. 1. The quilt center should now be 46½" square including seam allowances.

## add border Nos. 2–4

**1** Cut and piece remaining assorted red print 2½×42" strips to make:
- 2—2½×50½" border No. 2 strips
- 2—2½×46½" border No. 2 strips

**2** Join short border No. 2 strips to opposite edges of quilt center. Add long border No. 2 strips to remaining edges. Press all seams toward border No. 2. The quilt center should now be 50½" square including seam allowances.

**3** Cut and piece remaining assorted blue print 2½×42" strips to make:
- 2—2½×54½" border No. 3 strips
- 2—2½×50½" border No. 3 strips

**4** Join short border No. 3 strips to opposite edges of quilt center. Add long border No. 3 strips to remaining edges. Press all seams toward border No. 3. The quilt center should now be 54½" square including seam allowances.

**5** Cut and piece brown check 4½×42" strips to make:
- 2—4½×62½" border No. 4 strips
- 2—4½×54½" border No. 4 strips

**6** Join short border No. 4 strips to opposite edges of quilt center. Add long border No. 4 strips to remaining edges to complete quilt top. Press all seams toward border No. 4.

## finish quilt

**1** Layer quilt top, batting, and backing; baste. (For details, see Complete Quilt, *page 175*.)

**2** Quilt as desired. Machine-quilter Maryann Nelson stitched allover, edge-to-edge feather designs across the quilt top.

**3** Bind with mottled red binding strips. (For details, see Complete Quilt.)

# A PLACE FOR everything

Sew-as-you-go
place mats fit nicely into
a matching pieced holder
for storage or gift-giving.

DESIGNER **JULIE HERMAN**
(jaybirdquilts.com)

## materials *for four place mats and one holder*

- 1⅝ yards prequilted blue tone-on-tone (place mats, holder, holder flap) (See Select Fabrics, *right*)
- 29—2½×42" precut strips *or* 1⅔ yards total assorted prints in pink, green, yellow, and blue (place mats, holder flap, bindings, button loop)
- 1"-diameter flower button: orange

Finished place mat: 18×12"
Finished holder: 20×16" (closed)

Quantities are for precut 2½×42" strips and 44/45"-wide, 100% cotton fabrics.
Measurements include ¼" seam allowances. Sew with right sides together unless otherwise stated.

## select fabrics

The featured prequilted fabric has a blue tone-on-tone on one side (shown on place mats, *opposite*) and a brown animal print on the reverse side (shown on holder, *above*).

## cut fabrics

Cut pieces in the following order.

**From prequilted blue tone-on-tone, cut:**

- 1—17½×40" rectangle for holder
- 4—12×18" rectangles for place mats
- 1—10×12" rectangle for holder flap

**From assorted prints, cut:**

- 2—2½×42" binding strips for holder
- 12—2½×24" binding strips for place mats
- 15—2½×13" strips for place mats and holder flap
- 1—2½×6" strip for button loop

## assemble place mats

**1** Lay a prequilted 12×18" rectangle with blue tone-on-tone side facing up.

**2** Referring to **Diagram 1**, center an assorted print 2½×13" strip right side down 6" from a short edge of prequilted rectangle. Pin through all layers.

**3** Using a walking foot, stitch along right-hand edge of strip through all layers. Flip open strip to right side and press.

**4** Center a second assorted print 2½×13" strip atop first strip with right sides together, aligning raw edges. Pin through all layers.

**5** Stitch along right-hand edge of second strip through all layers (**Diagram 2**). Flip open second strip and press.

**6** With right sides together, center and align a third assorted print 2½×13" strip along right-hand edge of second strip. Stitch, flip, and

press as before (**Diagram 3**). Baste raw edge of third strip to right-hand edge of prequilted rectangle using a scant ¼" seam (**Diagram 4**).

**7** Referring to **Diagram 4**, trim strips along long edges of prequilted rectangle to complete place mat. The place mat should be 18×12".

**8** Using diagonal seams, sew together three assorted print 2½×24" binding strips to make a pieced binding strip. Bind place mat with pieced binding strip. (For details, see Complete Quilt, *page 175*.)

**9** Repeat steps 1–8 to make four place mats total.

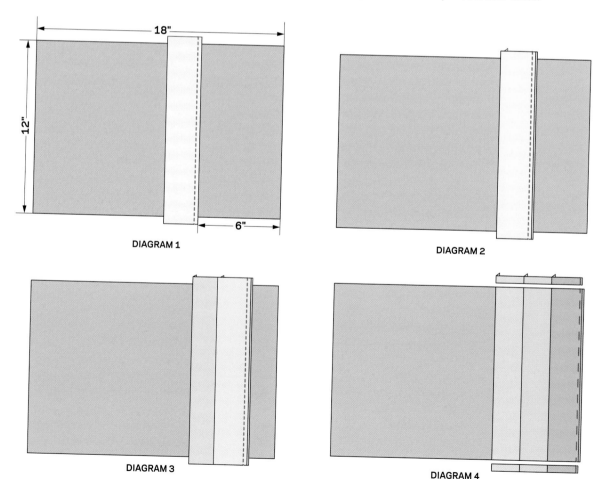

DIAGRAM 1

DIAGRAM 2

DIAGRAM 3

DIAGRAM 4

## assemble holder flap

**1** Using prequilted blue tone-on-tone 10×12" rectangle and three assorted print 2½×13" strips, repeat Assemble Place Mats, steps 1–7, to make holder flap (**Diagram 5**). The flap should be 10×12" including seam allowances.

**DIAGRAM 6**

**3** Using matching thread, topstitch along folded edges of strip (**Diagram 6**).

**4** Referring to **Diagram 7**, fold topstitched strip diagonally twice, aligning raw edges, to make a triangle on opposite end; press. Sew across base of triangle to make button loop. The loop should be about 3" long.

**DIAGRAM 8**

**6** Referring to **Diagram 9** and using one assorted print 2½×42" binding strip, bind flap along both short edges and the long edge with basted button loop; do not bind long edge opposite the loop. (For details, see Complete Quilt, page 175.)

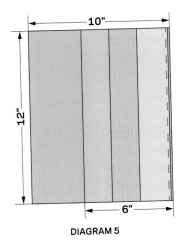

**DIAGRAM 5**

**DIAGRAM 7**

**2** Fold long edges of assorted print 2½×6" strip under ¼" with wrong side inside; press (**Diagram 6**). Fold strip in half lengthwise, aligning folded edges, and press. The folded strip should be 1" wide.

**5** Aligning raw edges, center and baste button loop to wrong side of flap (the side with animal print) on one long edge (**Diagram 8**).

**DIAGRAM 9**

··· *tip* ···

*The holder serves as a wrap when presenting the place mats*
*as a gift and provides stylish storage for the place mats.*
*Or, use the holder to protect a 9×13" or 10×15" baking dish*
*when you attend a potluck or family get-together.*

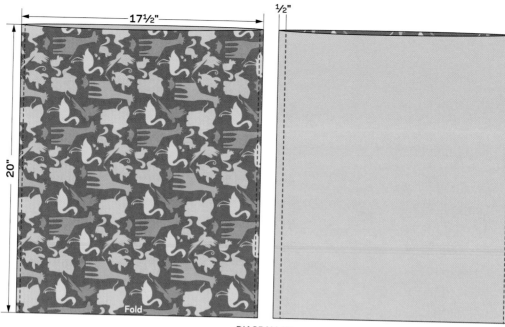

**DIAGRAM 10**

## finish holder

**1** Aligning short edges, fold prequilted 17½×40" rectangle in half with blue tone-on-tone inside to make a 17½×20" piece. Sew together long edges using a scant ¼" seam (Diagram 10).

**2** Turn blue tone-on-tone to outside and press. Topstitch ½" from each long edge to enclose raw edges (Diagram 10).

**3** Turn blue tone-on-tone to inside again and press to make holder body.

**4** Aligning raw edges, center and baste flap, wrong side up, to one short edge of holder body (Diagram 11).

**5** Bind raw edge of holder body with remaining assorted print 2½×42" binding strip (Diagram 11). (For details, see Complete Quilt, *page 175*.)

**5** Referring to Diagram 11, center and hand-sew button about 8" from open end (on side without flap) to complete holder (see tip, *opposite*). Insert place mats, close flap, and secure with button.

**DIAGRAM 11**

Before you attach the button, insert place mats or pan into holder and mark appropriate placement of the button.

## COLOR OPTION

An endearing wedding gift, this set of four place mats and coordinated holder comes together quickly using prequilted fabrics and precut strips. Sophisticated floral, paisley, and tone-on-tone fabrics display a muted texture that beckons an assortment of place settings.

Alternate precut 2½"-wide strips and 1½"-wide strips to make a beautiful batik wall hanging.

INSPIRED BY **CHERRY DELIGHT** FROM DESIGNER **JOANNA FIGUEROA OF FIG TREE & CO.** (figtreequilts.com)

# bird's-eye
# view

## materials

- ½ yard purple batik (quilt top)
- 22 to 24—1½×42" precut strips or 1⅛ yards cream batik (quilt top)
- 40—2½×42" precut strips or 3 yards total assorted batiks in green, blue, dark red, and brown (quilt top)
- ⅝ yard green batik (binding)
- 3⅝ yards backing fabric
- 64×69" batting

Finished quilt: 55½×60½"

**Quantities** are for precut 1½×42" and 2½×42" strips and 44/45"-wide, 100% cotton fabrics.
**Measurements** include ¼" seam allowances. Sew with right sides together unless otherwise stated.

## cut fabrics

Cut pieces in the following order.

**From purple batik, cut:**

- 1—9½×12½" rectangle

**From remaining purple batik, piece and cut:**

- 2—1½×60½" strips for Position 32
- 2—1½×53½" strips for Position 31

**From cream batik 1½×42" strips, piece and cut:**

- 2—1½×54½" strips for Position 28
- 2—1½×47½" strips for Position 27
- 2—1½×42½" strips for Position 21
- 2—1½×41½" strips for Position 23

- 2—1½×36½" strips for Position 17
- 2—1½×35½" strips for Position 18
- 2—1½×30½" strips for Position 13
- 2—1½×29½" strips for Position 14
- 2—1½×24½" strips for Position 9
- 2—1½×23½" strips for Position 10
- 2—1½×18½" strips for Position 5
- 2—1½×17½" strips for Position 6
- 2—1½×12½" strips for Position 1
- 2—1½×11½" strips for Position 2

**From assorted green, blue, dark red, and brown batik 2½×42" strips, piece and cut:**
- 2—2½×58½" strips for Position 30
- 2—2½×52½" strips for Position 26
- 2—2½×49½" strips for Position 29
- 2—1½×48½" strips for Position 24
- 2—2½×43½" strips for Position 25
- 2—2½×41½" strips for Position 22
- 2—2½×39½" strips for Position 20
- 2—2½×38½" strips for Position 19
- 2—2½×33½" strips for Position 16
- 2—2½×32½" strips for Position 15
- 2—2½×27½" strips for Position 12
- 2—2½×26½" strips for Position 11
- 2—2½×21½" strips for Position 8
- 2—2½×20½" strips for Position 7

- 2—2½×15½" strips for Position 4
- 2—2½×14½" strips for Position 3

**From green batik, cut:**
- 6—2½×42" binding strips

## assemble quilt top

1 Sew Position 1 cream batik 1½×12½" strips to long edges of purple batik 9½×12½" rectangle (**Diagram 1**). Press seams toward strips.

2 Join Position 2 cream batik 1½×11½" strips to remaining edges of purple batik rectangle (**Diagram 2**). Press seams toward strips.

**DIAGRAM 1**

**DIAGRAM 2**

**QUILT ASSEMBLY DIAGRAM**

**3** Referring to **Quilt Assembly Diagram** for placement, continue adding cream batik strips and assorted green, blue, dark red, and brown batik strips in same manner and in numerical order to complete quilt top.

## finish quilt

**1** Layer quilt top, batting, and backing; baste. (For details, see Complete Quilt, *page 175.*)

**2** Quilt as desired. Machine-quilter Nancy Sharr stitched large swirls across the quilt top.

**3** Bind with green batik binding strips. (For details, see Complete Quilt.)

Simple rectangles
lend brilliant color to a
stash-busting queen-size
quilt. What could
be easier?

# the.
# main
# event

DESIGNER **KATHIE HOLLAND**

## materials

- 83 to 90—1½×42" precut
  strips *or* 3½ yards total
  assorted red and brown
  prints, solids, and florals
  (pieced rows)
- 7⅝ yards* red floral stripe
  (sashing, border)
  * You will need 5⅛ yards if
  you are using an allover print
  or solid instead of fussy-
  cutting a border stripe
- ⅞ yard total assorted red
  prints (binding)
- 8¼ yards backing fabric
- 100×99" batting

**Finished quilt:** 92×90½"

**Quantities** are for precut
1½×42" strips and 44/45"-
wide, 100% cotton fabrics.
**Measurements** include ¼"
seam allowances. Sew with
right sides together unless
otherwise stated.

## cut fabrics

Cut pieces in the following order. Cut sashing and border strips lengthwise (parallel to the selvages). For the featured quilt, the sashing and border strips were fussy-cut from a floral stripe with a repeat every 8".

**From assorted red and brown prints, solids, and florals, cut:**
- 990—1½×3½" rectangles

**From red floral stripe, fussy-cut:**
- 2—8½×90½" border strips
- 10—4¾×90½" sashing strips

**From assorted red prints, cut:**
- Enough 2½"-wide strips to total 442" in length for binding

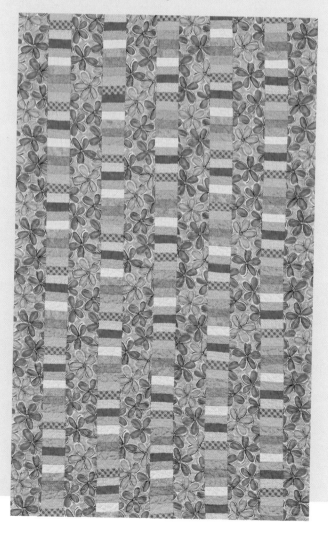

## COLOR OPTION

This pint-size version of *The Main Event* makes a perfect baby quilt or one for a toddler to snuggle under.

To duplicate the 41×58½" quilt, choose a print for the sashing strips first, then select nine complementary prints for the small rectangles. When using fewer fabrics in the pieced rows, it's faster to sew long strips together into a strip set before cutting them into 3½"-wide units.

## assemble pieced rows

Referring to photo, *opposite*, lay out 90 assorted red and brown print 1½×3½" rectangles in a row. Sew together rectangles to make a pieced row; press seams in one direction. The pieced row should be 3½×90½" including seam allowances. Repeat to make 11 pieced rows total.

## assemble quilt top

**1** Referring to photo, *opposite*, lay out red floral stripe border strips, pieced rows, and red floral stripe sashing strips in 23 rows.

**2** Sew together rows and strips to complete quilt top. Press seams toward sashing and border strips.

## finish quilt

**1** Layer quilt top, batting, and backing; baste. (For details, see Complete Quilt, *page 175*.)

**2** Quilt as desired. Machine-quilter Karen Gilson stitched allover free-form feather and swirl patterns. She accented the outer edge of each red floral border strip with an orange petal design, mimicking the floral vine motif.

**3** Using diagonal seams, sew together assorted red print 2½"-wide strips to make a pieced binding strip. Bind quilt with pieced binding strip. (For details, see Complete Quilt.)

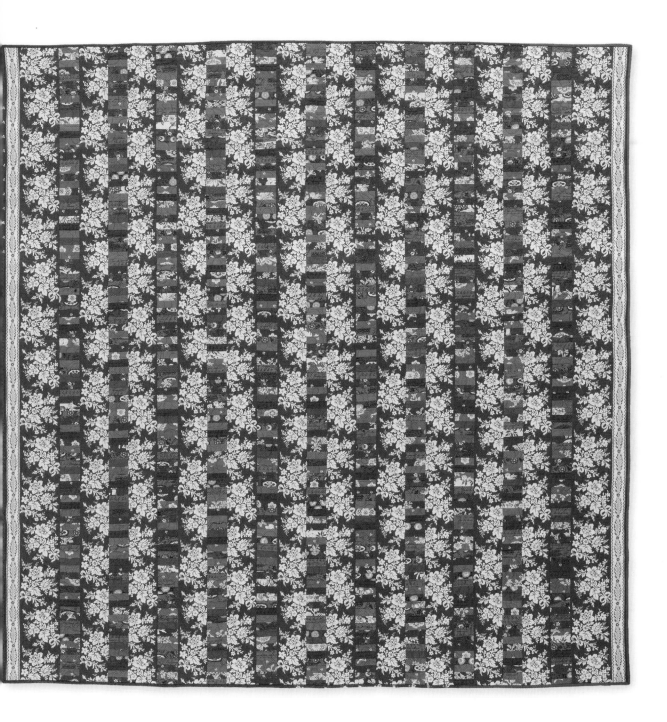

*Whenever you finish a project, cut the remaining fabric into assorted-width strips and store them in baskets that are clearly marked with the strip width. Over time, you will collect an assortment you can turn into a scrappy quilt top, pillow, or table runner.*

Raw-edge appliqué flowers add a homespun look to a foundation stitched from 2½"-wide strips.

# daisy duo

DESIGNER **LYNNE HAGMEIER OF KANSAS TROUBLES QUILTERS** (ktquilts.com)

## materials

- 6—2½×42" precut strips *or* ½ yard green print No. 1 (appliqué foundation, binding)
- 4—2½×42" precut strips *each or* ⅜ yard *each* of assorted tan prints Nos. 1-3 (appliqué foundation)
- 1—2½×42" precut strip *each or* ⅛ yard *each* of assorted green prints Nos. 2-5 (appliqué foundation)
- 18×22" piece (fat quarter) green plaid (stem and leaf appliqués)
- 2—9×22" pieces (fat eighths) assorted gold plaids (petal appliqués)
- 1¾ yards backing fabric
- 30×62" batting
- Freezer paper
- 4—¾"-diameter buttons: brown

Finished table runner: 22×54"

Quantities are for precut 2½×42" strips and 44/45"-wide, 100% cotton fabrics.
Measurements include ¼" seam allowances. Sew with right sides together unless otherwise stated.

## cut fabrics

Cut pieces in the following order.
Patterns are on *Pattern Sheet 1*. To use freezer paper to cut A and B appliqués, complete the following steps.

1 Lay freezer paper, shiny side down, over patterns A and B. Use a pencil to trace each pattern the number of times indicated in cutting instructions, leaving ½" between tracings. Cut out freezer-paper shapes roughly ¼" outside drawn lines.

2 Using a hot, dry iron, press freezer-paper shapes, shiny sides down, onto wrong sides of designated fabrics with long edges on the bias; let cool. Cut out fabric shapes on drawn lines. Peel off freezer paper.

**From green print No. 1, cut:**
- 4—2½×42" binding strips
- 4—2½×8½" rectangles (for rows 1 and 11)
- 1—2½×7¾" rectangle (for row 6)
- 1—2½×6¾" rectangle (for row 6)

**From tan print No. 1, cut:**
- 2—2½×42" strips (for rows 4 and 8)
- 2—2½×38½" strips (for rows 1 and 11)

**From tan print No. 2, cut:**
- 2—2½×42" strips (for rows 2 and 10)
- 2—2½×41" strips (for rows 5 and 7)

**From tan print No. 3, cut:**
- 2—2½×42" strips (for rows 3 and 9)
- 1—2½×41" strip (for row 6)

**From green print No. 2, cut:**
- 4—2½×6¾" rectangles (for rows 2 and 10)

**From green print No. 3, cut:**
- 2—2½×7½" rectangles (for rows 3 and 9)
- 2—2½×6" rectangles (for rows 3 and 9)

**From green print No. 4, cut:**
- 2—2½×7" rectangles (for rows 4 and 8)
- 2—2½×6½" rectangles (for rows 4 and 8)

**From green print No. 5, cut:**
- 2—2½×7¾" rectangles (for rows 5 and 7)
- 2—2½×6¾" rectangles (for rows 5 and 7)

**From green plaid, bias-cut:**
- 2—½×20" stem appliqués (For details, see Cut Bias Strips, *page 170*.)
- 2—⅜×20" stem appliqués
- 2—½×12½" stem appliqués
- 2—⅜×12½" stem appliqués
- 10 of Pattern B

**From *each* gold plaid fat eighth, bias-cut:**
- 10 of Pattern A

## quilt appliqué foundation

1 Layer appliqué foundation, batting, and backing; baste. (For details, see Complete Quilt, *page 175*.)

2 Quilt as desired. Machine-quilter Lois Sprecker stitched in the ditch between the tan print strips and green print rectangles.

## add raw-edge appliqués

1 Referring to Appliqué Placement Diagram, position ½"-wide stem appliqués in lengths indicated on quilted appliqué foundation. Center ⅜"-wide stem appliqués on top of wider stems, matching lengths; pin in place. Using matching thread, machine-straight-stitch down center of stem appliqués through all layers.

2 Referring to Appliqué Placement Diagram, position A and B pieces on quilted appliqué foundation; pin or

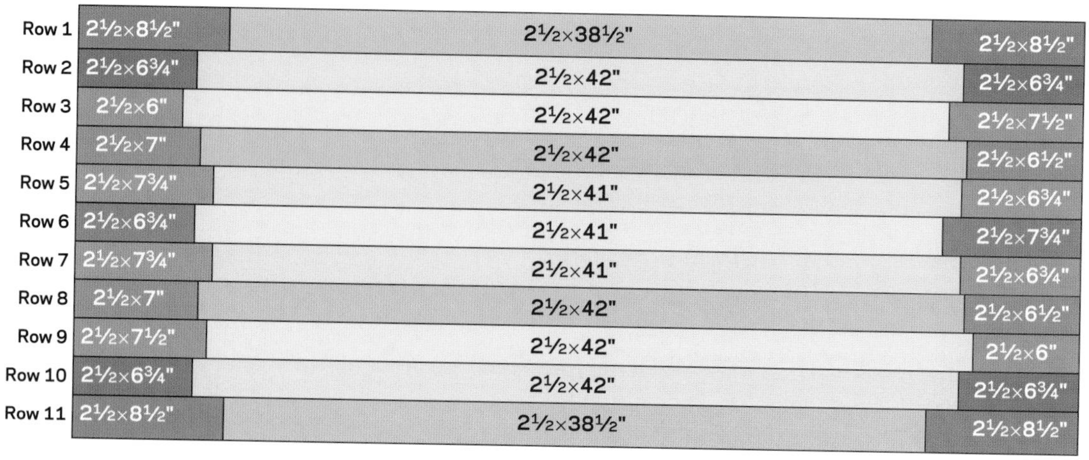

## assemble appliqué foundation

1 Referring to Table Runner Assembly Diagram, sew a green print No. 1—2½×8½" rectangle to each end of a tan print No. 1—2½×38½" strip to make row 1. Press seams toward rectangles. The row should be 2½×54½" including seam allowances.

2 Referring to Table Runner Assembly Diagram, repeat Step 1 using remaining green print rectangles and tan print strips to make rows 2–11.

3 Referring to Table Runner Assembly Diagram, sew together rows 1–11 to make appliqué foundation. Press seams in one direction. The appliqué foundation should be 22½×54½" including seam allowances.

| | Left | Center | Right |
|---|---|---|---|
| Row 1 | 2½×8½" | 2½×38½" | 2½×8½" |
| Row 2 | 2½×6¾" | 2½×42" | 2½×6¾" |
| Row 3 | 2½×6" | 2½×42" | 2½×7½" |
| Row 4 | 2½×7" | 2½×42" | 2½×6½" |
| Row 5 | 2½×7¾" | 2½×41" | 2½×6¾" |
| Row 6 | 2½×6¾" | 2½×41" | 2½×7¾" |
| Row 7 | 2½×7¾" | 2½×41" | 2½×6¾" |
| Row 8 | 2½×7" | 2½×42" | 2½×6½" |
| Row 9 | 2½×7½" | 2½×42" | 2½×6" |
| Row 10 | 2½×6¾" | 2½×42" | 2½×6¾" |
| Row 11 | 2½×8½" | 2½×38½" | 2½×8½" |

**TABLE RUNNER ASSEMBLY DIAGRAM**

baste in place. Using matching threads, machine-straight-stitch ⅛" from raw edges.

**3** Sew or tie a brown button to each flower center with matching thread.

## finish table runner
Bind table runner with green print No. 1 binding strips. (For details, see Complete Quilt.)

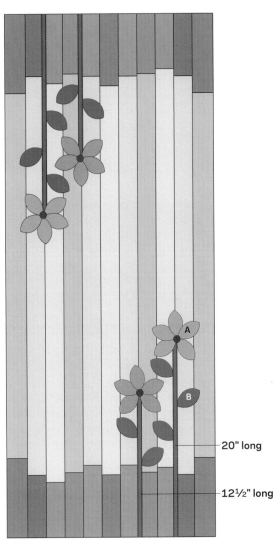

20" long

12½" long

**APPLIQUÉ PLACEMENT DIAGRAM**

# linked together

DESIGNER
**MONIQUE DILLARD OF OPEN GATE QUILTS**
(opengatequilts.com)

Grab precut 2½×42" strips in your favorite fabrics to devise an interesting illusion of interlocking squares and strips.

## materials

- 26—2½×42" precut strips *or* 1⅔ yards total assorted cream and gold prints (blocks, inner border)
- 19—2½×42" precut strips *or* 1¼ yards total assorted blue and green prints (blocks)
- 18—2½×42" precut strips *or* 1¼ yards total assorted olive green and pink prints (blocks)
- 10—2½×42" precut strips *or* ¾ yard total assorted brown prints (blocks)
- 1¾ yards pink floral (outer border, binding)
- 3⅞ yards backing fabric
- 69" square batting

**Finished quilt:** 61" square
**Finished block:** 8" square

**Quantities** are for precut 2½×42" strips and 44/45"-wide, 100% cotton fabrics.
**Measurements** include ¼" seam allowances. Sew with right sides together unless otherwise stated.

## cut fabrics

Cut pieces in the following order.

**From assorted cream and gold prints, cut:**
- 12—1¾×20" strips for inner border
- 288—2½" squares (36 sets of 8 matching squares)

**From assorted blue and green prints, cut 36 matching sets of:**
- 2—2½×4½" rectangles
- 4—2½" squares

**From assorted olive green and pink prints, cut:**
- 144—2½×4½" rectangles (36 sets of 4 matching rectangles)

**From assorted brown prints, cut:**
- 144—2½" squares (36 sets of 4 matching squares)

**From pink floral, cut:**
- 7—5½×42" strips for outer border
- 7—2½×42" binding strips

## assemble blocks

1 For one block, gather eight matching cream or gold print 2½" squares, a set of matching blue or green print pieces (two 2½×4½" rectangles and four 2½" squares), four matching olive green or pink print 2½×4½" rectangles, and four matching brown print 2½" squares.

2 Use a pencil to mark a diagonal line on wrong sides of cream or gold print 2½" squares and blue or green print 2½" squares. (To prevent fabric from stretching as you draw lines, place 220-grit sandpaper under squares.)

3 Align a marked cream or gold print square with one end of a blue or green print 2½×4½" rectangle (**Diagram 1**; note direction of marked line). Sew on marked line; trim seam allowance to ¼". Press open attached triangle, pressing seam away from cream or gold print.

**DIAGRAM 1**

4 Align a second marked cream or gold print square with opposite end of Step 3 rectangle (**Diagram 1**). Stitch, trim, and press as before to make a Flying Geese unit. The unit should be 4½×2½" including seam allowances.

5 Repeat steps 3 and 4 to make a second Flying Geese unit.

6 Align a marked cream or gold print square with left-hand end of an olive green or pink print 2½×4½" rectangle (**Diagram 2**; note direction of marked line). Stitch, trim, and press as in Step 3.

**DIAGRAM 2**

7 Align a marked blue or green print square with right-hand end of Step 6 rectangle (**Diagram 2**; again note direction of marked line). Stitch, trim, and press as before to make a diagonal unit. The diagonal unit should be 4½×2½" including seam allowances.

8 Repeat steps 6 and 7 to make four diagonal units total.

9 Referring to **Diagram 3**, sew together a Flying Geese unit, a diagonal unit, and two brown print 2½" squares in two rows. Press seams toward brown print squares. Join rows; press seam toward row with diagonal unit. Add a diagonal unit to left-hand edge of joined rows to make a block segment (**Diagram 4**). Press seam away from diagonal unit. The block segment should be 8½×4½" including seam allowances. Repeat to make a second block segment.

**DIAGRAM 3**

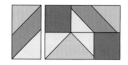

**DIAGRAM 4**

10 Referring to **Diagram 5**, join block segments to make a block. Press seam open. The block should be 8½" square including seam allowances.

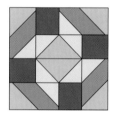

**DIAGRAM 5**

11 Repeat steps 1–10 to make 36 blocks total.

## assemble quilt center

1 Referring to **Quilt Assembly Diagram**, lay out blocks in six rows. Sew together blocks in each row. Press seams in one direction, alternating direction with each row.

2 Join rows to make quilt center. Press seams in one direction. The quilt center should be 48½" square including seam allowances.

## assemble and add borders

1 Using diagonal seams, cut and piece assorted cream and gold print 1¾×20" strips to make:
- 2—1¾×51" inner border strips
- 2—1¾×48½" inner border strips

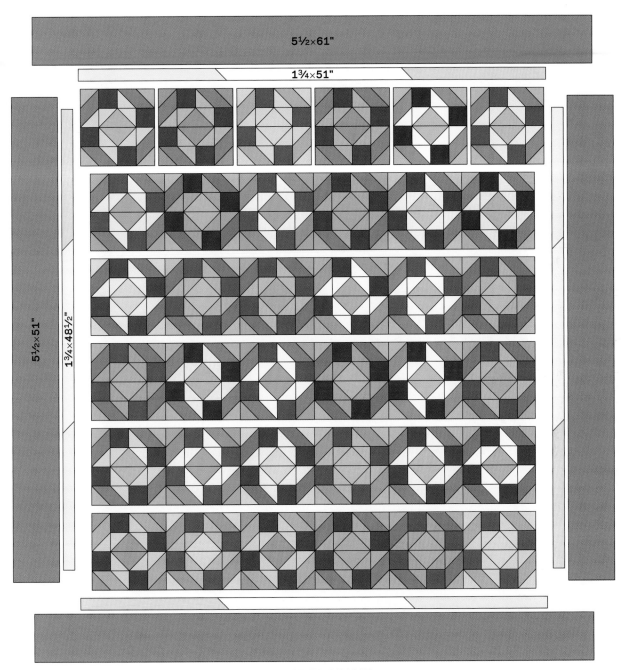

5½×61"

1¾×51"

5½×51"

1¾×48½"

**QUILT ASSEMBLY DIAGRAM**

**2** Sew short inner border strips to opposite edges of quilt center. Add long inner border strips to remaining edges. Press all seams toward inner border.

**3** Cut and piece pink floral 5½×42" strips to make:
- 2—5½×61" outer border strips
- 2—5½×51" outer border strips

**4** Sew short outer border strips to opposite edges of quilt center. Add long outer border strips to remaining edges to complete quilt top. Press all seams toward outer border.

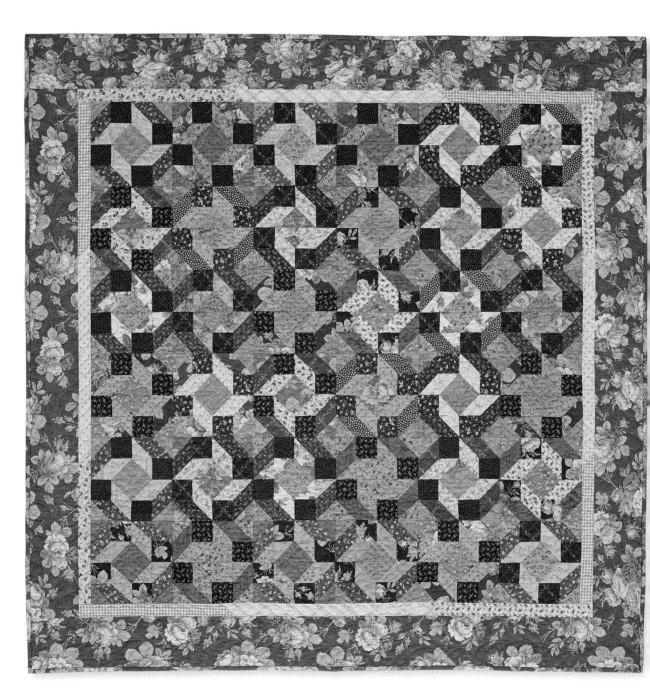

··· tip ···

*"When I design quilts using precut fabrics, I try to use as much of the fabric as I can. To use up leftover precut strips, I often piece them together to make a scrappy binding. The precut 2½" width is perfect!"*

—DESIGNER MONIQUE DILLARD

## finish quilt

1 Layer quilt top, batting, and backing; baste. (For details, see Complete Quilt, *page 175*.)

2 Quilt as desired. Sue Glorch machine-quilted an allover stipple across the quilt center and added feather designs in the borders (**Quilting Diagram**).

3 Bind with pink floral binding strips. (For details, see Complete Quilt.)

QUILTING DIAGRAM

# COLOR OPTION

Watch new shapes emerge as you tweak the color placement of *Linked Together*. By using the same batik for the rectangles in the diagonal units and the 2½" squares in the block segments, quilt tester Laura Boehnke made the spinning pinwheels prominent. A tan batik in the inner border and each block corner unifies the design.

Precut batik 2½"-wide strips help achieve the look. "The mottled prints blend when you piece them together, resulting in a seamless appearance," Laura says.

Tempted by rolls of assorted 2½"-wide fabric strips at your local quilt shop? Put a roll to good use as you stitch this trendy table runner.

# *on a* ROLL

DESIGNER **MARTI MICHELL OF FROM MARTI MICHELL** (frommarti.com)

## materials

- 7—2½×42" precut strips *or* ½ yard total assorted blue prints
- 3—2½×42" precut strips *or* ¼ yard total assorted pink prints
- 7—2½×42" precut strips *or* ½ yard total assorted brown prints
- 3—2½×42" precut strips *or* ¼ yard total assorted green prints
- 1¼ yards backing fabric
- 16½×45" thin batting

**Finished table runner:** 16×44½"

**Quantities** are for precut 2½×42" strips and 44/45"-wide, 100% cotton fabrics. **Measurements** include ¼" seam allowances. Sew with right sides together unless otherwise stated.

## designer notes

Designer Marti Michell cut more diamonds than needed so she could mix and match them while piecing the table runner top.

## cut fabrics

Cut pieces in the following order.

The Diamond Pattern is on *Pattern Sheet 1*. To make a template of the Diamond Pattern, see Make and Use Templates, *page 171*.

To save time when cutting, use designer Marti Michell's acrylic diamond template (turn to *page 111* to see template in use). To make sure the diamonds' grain lines all run crosswise on the finished table runner, Marti recommends leaving each 2½"-wide strip folded in half when you cut the diamonds. Use diamonds cut from the top layer of each strip for the odd-numbered rows of the table runner top and those cut from the bottom layer for the even-numbered rows.

**From assorted blue prints, cut:**
- 4—2½×16" strips
- 2—2½×14" strips
- 2—2½×11" strips
- 17 of Diamond Pattern

**From assorted pink prints, cut:**
- 17 of Diamond Pattern

**From assorted brown prints, cut:**
- 3—2½×15" strips
- 4—2½×13" strips
- 1—2½×8" strip
- 17 of Diamond Pattern

**From assorted green prints, cut:**
- 18 of Diamond Pattern

**From backing fabric, cut:**
- 1—16½×45" rectangle

## assemble table runner top

1  Referring to **Quilt Assembly Diagram**, arrange pieces in eight rows; one end of each blue print and brown print strip will be angled later. (The direction of the diamond pieces alternates with each row to create a chevron pattern.)

2  Once satisfied with your arrangement, use one edge of the Diamond Pattern or the 60° line on a ruler to mark and cut the appropriate angle at one end of each blue print and brown print strip **(Cutting Diagram)**.

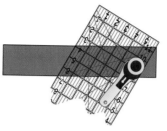

**CUTTING DIAGRAM**

3  Sew together pieces in each row. Press seams in one direction, alternating direction with each row.

4  Join rows to complete table runner top. Press seams in one direction. Trim table runner top to 16½×45" including seam allowances.

## finish table runner

1  Baste batting rectangle to wrong side of table runner top, machine-stitching a scant ¼" from edges. Trim batting close to stitching, especially around the corners.

| | |
|---|---|
| 2½×13" | 2½×11" |
| 2½×13" | 2½×14" |
| 2½×13" | 2½×16" |
| 2½×15" | 2½×16" |
| 2½×8" | 2½×16" |
| 2½×15" | 2½×11" |
| 2½×15" | 2½×14" |
| 2½×13" | 2½×16" |

**QUILT ASSEMBLY DIAGRAM**

*Want to be ready to whip up this oh-so-easy runner as a gift any time of the year? Start by creating a stash of your own strips. Every time you buy new fabric, cut a 2½" strip and set it aside in a clearly marked, see-through bag. In no time you'll see your strip stash grow into a stack big enough to create another runner.*

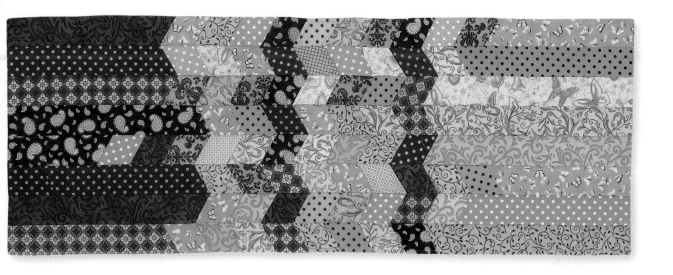

## ···tip···

*To make* On a Roll *in a different size, add additional rows to the runner's width. Or, for an extra-long runner, repeat the design twice end to end, placing an additional chevron segment in the center between the two repeats.*

# Acrylic Templates Save Time

With a passion for teaching techniques and shortcuts that make quilting easier and more fun, designer Marti Michell ( frommarti.com) has designed quilt patterns and notions for more than 30 years.

Inspired by rolls of precut fabric strips, Marti created

acrylic 2½" Stripper Templates to cut various shapes (including 45° and 60° diamonds, hexagons, and equilateral triangles) from 2½"-wide

fabric strips with virtually no waste. Marti used the templates, above, to cut the 60° diamonds for this project.

**2** With right sides together, layer table runner top and backing rectangle. Sew together, leaving a 6" opening for turning. Turn table runner right side out through opening; press. Hand-sew opening closed.

**3** Quilt as desired. Marti and machine-quilter Harriett Fox stitched in the ditch along each horizontal and vertical seam line. On three of the vertical zigzag rows at the

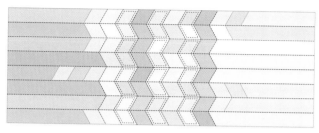

QUILTING DIAGRAM

center, they outlined a chevron pattern over pairs of diamonds, stitching ¼" inside the seam lines (Quilting Diagram).

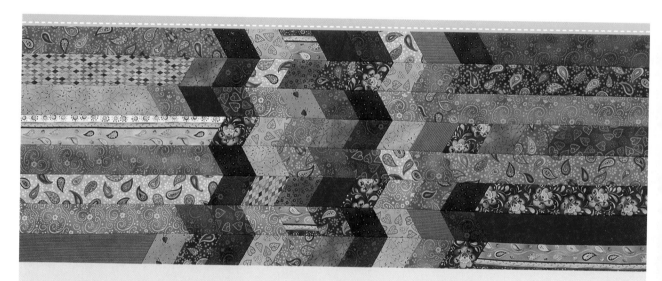

# COLOR OPTION

This easy table runner design will take you through the whole year. Quilt tester Laura Boehnke made a version perfect for late summer or autumn.

"To keep the flow of color consistent in the zigzags on the table runner, I made sure to use more tone-on-tone fabrics for the diamonds and fewer multicolor or large prints," Laura says. "Otherwise, the chevrons could be lost in the overall design."

# regal
## TREATMENT

It's sew easy! Whip up a cozy throw in no time using precut batik strips in shades of purple for a royal touch.

INSPIRED BY MIXED BERRIES FROM DESIGNER **KIMBERLY WALUS**
(bittybitsandpieces.blogspot.com)

## materials

- 26—2½×42" precut strips *or* 2 yards total assorted light batiks in lavender and lilac (blocks)
- 26—2½×42" precut strips *or* 2 yards total assorted dark batiks in purple and violet-blue (blocks)
- ⅝ yard violet batik (inner border)
- 1⅞ yards dark purple batik (outer border)
- ⅔ yard purple batik (binding)
- 4⅝ yards backing fabric
- 82" square batting

**Finished quilt:** 73½" square
**Finished blocks:** 10" square

**Quantities** are for 44/45"-wide, 100% cotton fabrics.
**Measurements** include ¼" seam allowances. Sew with right sides together unless otherwise stated.

## cut fabrics

Cut pieces in the following order.
**From one light batik, cut:**
- 18—2½" squares

**From remaining assorted light batiks, cut:**
- 72—2½×10½" rectangles
- 36—2½×4½" rectangles (18 sets of 2 matching rectangles)

**From one dark batik, cut:**
- 18—2½" squares

**From remaining assorted dark batiks, cut:**
- 72—2½×10½" rectangles
- 36—2½×4½" rectangles (18 sets of 2 matching rectangles)

**From violet batik, cut:**
- 7—2½×42" strips for inner border

**From dark purple batik, cut:**
- 8—5×42" strips for outer border

**From purple batik, cut:**
- 8—2½×42" binding strips

## assemble blocks

1  Join a light batik 2½" square and two matching dark batik 2½×4½" rectangles to make a dark center rectangle unit (**Diagram 1**). Press seams toward dark batik. The unit should be 2½×10½" including seam allowances. Repeat to make 18 dark center rectangle units total.

**DIAGRAM 1**

2  Referring to **Diagram 2**, lay out four assorted dark batik 2½×10½" rectangles and one dark center rectangle unit in horizontal rows. Join rows to make a dark block. Press seams away from center rectangle unit. The block should be 10½" square including seam allowances. Repeat to make 18 dark blocks total.

**DIAGRAM 2**

3  Using dark batik 2½" squares and assorted light batik 2½×4½" rectangle sets, repeat Step 1 to make 18 light center rectangle units.

4  Using assorted light batik 2½×10½" rectangles and dark center rectangle units, repeat Step 2 to make 18 light blocks.

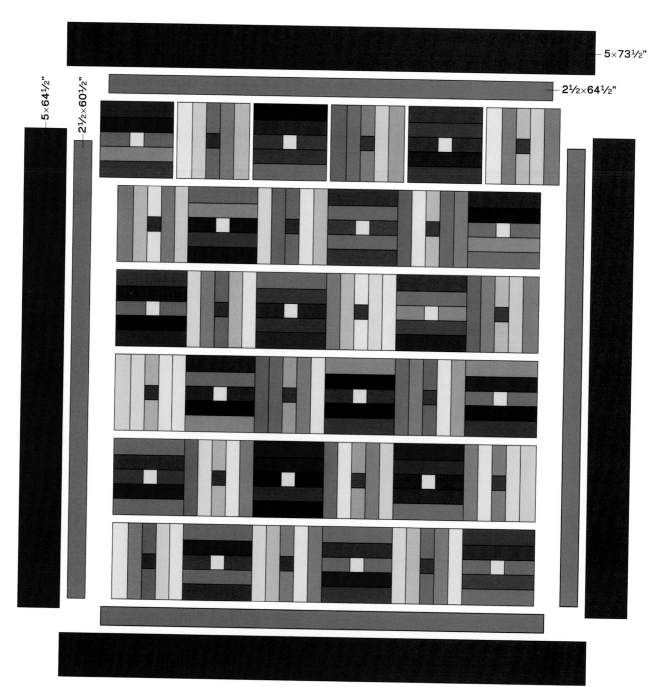

5×73½"

2½×64½"

5×64½"

2½×60½"

QUILT ASSEMBLY DIAGRAM

*Use a 70/10 machine needle when piecing and quilting batik fabrics. Because batiks have a denser weave than regular cotton fabrics, this slightly finer needle is ideal.*

## assemble quilt center

1 Referring to **Quilt Assembly Diagram**, alternate blocks in six horizontal rows, rotating light blocks 90° as shown.

2 Sew together blocks in each row. Press seams in one direction, alternating direction with each row. Join rows to make quilt center. Press seams in one direction. The quilt center should be 60½" square including seam allowances.

## assemble and add borders

1 Cut and piece violet batik 2½×42" strips to make:
   - 2—2½×64½" inner border strips
   - 2—2½×60½" inner border strips

2 Join short inner border strips to opposite edges of quilt center. Add long inner border strips to remaining edges. Press all seams toward inner border.

3 Cut and piece dark purple batik 5×42" strips to make:
   - 2—5×73½" outer border strips
   - 2—5×64½" outer border strips

4 Join short outer border strips to opposite edges of quilt center. Add long outer border strips to remaining edges to complete quilt top. Press all seams toward outer border.

## finish quilt

1 Layer quilt top, batting, and backing; baste. (For details, see Complete Quilt, *page 175*.)

2 Quilt as desired. Nancy Sharr stitched an allover flower pattern on the featured quilt.

3 Bind with purple batik binding strips. (For details, see Complete Quilt.)

# squares

# fly.into spring

Orderly rows of Flying Geese units take flight amid meandering vine appliqués for a stunning play on opposites. Unify the look with an easy-to-make scalloped edge.

DESIGNER **ELEANOR BURNS OF QUILT IN A DAY** (quiltinaday.com)

## materials

See "Tools Make It Easy," *page 123*, for designer Eleanor Burns' advice on using a specialty ruler and template.

- 30—10" precut squares *or* 2½ yards total assorted prints (Flying Geese units, flower appliqués)
- 6¼ yards solid white (Flying Geese units, sashing, border)
- 3—10" precut squares *or* ⅓ yard total assorted solids (flower center appliqués)
- 2 yards green print (leaf and vine appliqués, binding)
- 5⅝ yards backing fabric
- 84×100" batting
- 3 yards lightweight fusible web
- 100% cotton, 12-weight thread to match or contrast appliqués
- Size 100/16 topstitch needle
- Air- or water-soluble marker

Finished quilt: 75¼×91¼"
Finished Flying Geese unit: 8×4"

**Quantities** are for precut 10" squares and 44/45"-wide, 100% cotton fabrics. **Measurements** include ¼" seam allowances. Sew with right sides together unless otherwise stated.

## cut fabrics

To plan this quilt in your own colorway, use the **Coloring Diagram** on *Pattern Sheet 2*.

Patterns are on *Pattern Sheet 1*. To use fusible web for appliquéing, complete the following steps.

To save time, Eleanor used an AccuQuilt die-cutting machine (*accuquilt.com*) to cut appliqué pieces for the featured quilt. If using this tool, fuse fusible web to the backs of the fabrics before cutting.

**1** Lay fusible web, paper side up, over patterns. Use a pencil to trace each pattern the number of times indicated in cutting instructions, leaving ½" between tracings. Cut out each fusible-web shape roughly ¼" outside traced lines.

**2** Following the manufacturer's instructions, press each fusible-web shape onto wrong side of designated fabric; let cool. Cut out fabric shapes on drawn lines. Peel off paper backings.

Cut pieces in the following order.
**From assorted print
10" squares, cut:**
- 18—9½" squares
- 24 *each* of patterns A and B

**From solid white, cut:**
- 9—10½×42" strips for border
- 6—8½×42" strips for sashing
- 18—11" squares

**From assorted solid
10" squares, cut:**
- 24 of Pattern C

**From green print, cut:**
- 1—16×42" rectangle, cutting it into 9—1¼×22" bias strips (For details, see Cut Bias Strips, *page 170*.)
- 2—16×42" rectangles, cutting them into 16—2¼×22" bias binding strips
- 69 of Pattern D

## assemble flying geese units

**1** With right sides together, center each assorted print 9½" square on a solid white 11" square; press.

**2** Place a 6×24" acrylic ruler diagonally on a pair of layered squares so the ruler touches all four corners. Use an air- or water-soluble marker to mark a diagonal line (Diagram 1). Repeat on all layered squares.

**DIAGRAM 1**

**3** Using a short stitch length, sew each pair of layered squares together with two seams, stitching ¼" on each side of drawn line (Diagram 2). Eleanor recommends sewing 15 stitches per inch (a stitch length of 2.0).

To save time, chain-piece, or assembly-line-sew, layered squares, machine-sewing pairs one after the other without lifting the presser foot or clipping threads between

pairs. First sew along one side of drawn lines, then turn group of pairs around and sew along other side of lines.

**4** Cut a pair apart on drawn line to make two triangle A units (Diagram 3). Open each triangle A unit and press seams toward solid white triangles to make two off-center triangle-squares (Diagram 4).

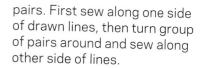

**DIAGRAM 2**

**DIAGRAM 3**

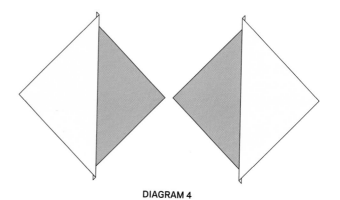

**DIAGRAM 4**

**5** Place off-center triangle-squares right sides together so each print triangle faces a solid white triangle. Match up outside edges (Diagram 5). Notice that there is a gap between seams; they should not "lock."

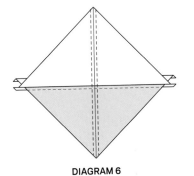

**DIAGRAM 6**

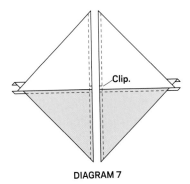

Clip.

**DIAGRAM 7**

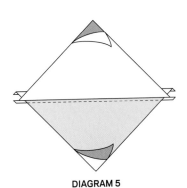

**DIAGRAM 5**

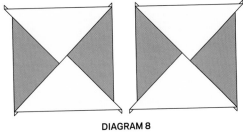

**DIAGRAM 8**

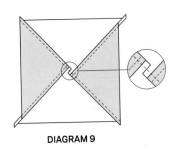

**DIAGRAM 9**

**6** Referring to **Diagram 6,** on layered triangle-squares mark a diagonal line perpendicular to existing seam. Sew together with two seams, stitching ¼" on each side of drawn line.

**7** Cut apart on drawn line to make two triangle B units. Clip center of seam allowances just up to stitching in order to press seams in opposite directions (Diagram 7).

**8** Open each triangle B unit to make two off-center hourglass units (Diagram 8). Press seams away from assorted print triangles; at clipped seam, you'll press fabric in opposite directions (Diagram 9).

# Tools Make It Easy

Take advantage of specialized products to make quilting more fun. For *Fly into Spring*, two acrylic tools from Quilt in a Day enable precise cutting and perfect placement. Use the Large Flying Geese Ruler **(Photo A)** to create 8×4" finished Flying Geese units in a snap. The Scallops, Vines & Waves Template has adjustable-length guidelines for marking the vine appliqués **(Photo B)** and scalloped border **(Photo C).**

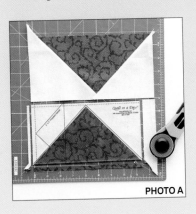

**PHOTO A**

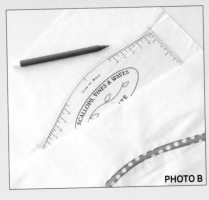

**PHOTO B**

**PHOTO C**

**9** Using an acrylic ruler, trim each off-center hourglass unit into two 8½×4½" Flying Geese units, making sure to leave a ¼" seam allowance at the peak of the Flying Geese (Diagram 10). (Eleanor used her Large Flying Geese Ruler for this step; see "Tools Make It Easy," *page 123*.)

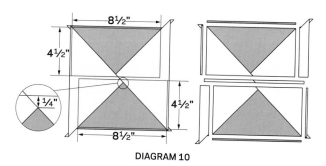

**DIAGRAM 10**

**10** Repeat steps 4–9 to make 72 Flying Geese units total (18 sets of four matching units).

## prepare sashing strip foundations

**1** Cut and piece solid white 8½×42" strips to make:
  - 3—8½×72½" sashing strips (Eleanor recommends cutting the strips ½" longer than specified to allow for shrinkage from appliqué.)

**2** With wrong sides together, fold a sashing strip in half lengthwise; press to mark center guideline. Open strip and place right side up. Make a mark on the center guideline

4¾" from top and bottom edges. Then mark every 9", making a total of eight marks (Diagram 11).

**3** Beginning at the top mark, draw a wavy line that is about 1" from the centerline at its widest point, alternating direction at each mark, to prepare a sashing strip foundation (Diagram 12). (Eleanor used her Scallops, Vines & Waves Template for this step; see "Tools Make It Easy," *page 123*.)

**4** Repeat steps 2 and 3 to prepare three sashing strip foundations total.

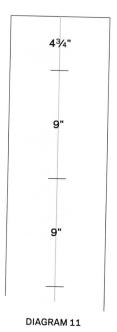

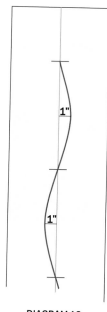

**DIAGRAM 11**          **DIAGRAM 12**

# Tips from Eleanor

- To "set" seams, press them flat (as they were stitched) before opening them and pressing them in the desired direction.

- When pressing units, make sure you open them all the way. Little folds or tucks in

seams can result in pieces that are too small.

- When appliquéing around curves with a blanket stitch, stop with your needle down in the fabric on the right-hand side of the stitch, then pivot the fabric.

- Finish outside edges of selected appliqués with the same color of thread before switching to the next thread. For ease in managing the long sashing strip foundations when appliquéing, roll the strip ends toward the area you are stitching.

## appliqué sashing strips

1  Sew together three green print 1¼×22" bias strips to make a vine strip. Press seams open. Repeat to make three vine strips total.

2  Press each vine strip in half with wrong sides together.

3  Referring to **Diagram 13**, position a vine strip on the wavy line on each sashing strip foundation. Sew a scant ¼" from vine strip raw edges. Trim excess vine. Turn vine strip over raw edges and press flat. Sew folded edge in place by hand or machine.

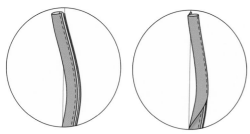

**DIAGRAM 13**

4  Center a C circle and a B flower on an A flower to make a flower stack. Repeat to make 24 flower stacks total.

5  Referring to **Quilt Assembly Diagram**, position eight flower stacks and 23 D leaves on each sashing strip foundation. Fuse in place following manufacturer's directions.

6  Set up your machine with a size 100/16 topstitch needle and a blanket stitch that is 3½ millimeters wide and 2½ millimeters long. In the needle use heavyweight thread in a shade slightly darker than the fabric or in a contrasting shade (Eleanor prefers Sulky 100% cotton, 12-weight thread). Use regular sewing thread in the bobbin. Blanket-stitch around each flower and leaf to appliqué three sashing strips.

## assemble quilt center

1  Lay out Flying Geese units in four vertical rows, using the same color pattern in each row. Sew together the units in rows.

   To easily keep all rows identical, assembly-line-sew the first two units in each row without clipping connecting threads. Add remaining Flying Geese units in same manner, then clip connecting threads. Press seams toward top of each row.

2  To stagger Flying Geese rows and create a stair-step effect as shown in **Quilt Assembly Diagram**, remove bottom Flying Geese unit from the second row and sew it to top of second row. From third row, remove bottom two Flying Geese units and sew them to top of third row. From fourth row, remove bottom three Flying Geese units and sew them to top of fourth row.

3  Referring to **Quilt Assembly Diagram**, sew together Flying Geese rows and sashing strips to make quilt center. Press seams toward sashing strips. The quilt center should be 56½×72½" including seam allowances.

## add border

1  Cut and piece solid white 10½×42" strips to make:
   - 2—10½×93½" border strips
   - 2—10½×77½" border strips

2  Beginning and ending seams ¼" from quilt center edges, sew long border strips to long edges of quilt center. Add short border strips to remaining edges, mitering corners, to complete quilt top. (For details, see Miter Borders, *page 174*.) Press all seams toward border.

## finish quilt

1  Layer quilt top, batting, and backing; baste. (For details, see Complete Quilt, *page 175*.)

2  A Full-Size Scallop Template for marking scallops on the border is on *Pattern Sheet 1*. To make a template, see Make and Use Templates, *page 171*.

**QUILT ASSEMBLY DIAGRAM**

**3** Referring to **Scallop Marking Diagram**, *Pattern Sheet 1,* mark eight scallops along border's top and bottom edges and 10 scallops along border's side edges, blending scallops to a gently rounded shape at each corner. Do not trim scallops yet.

**4** Quilt as desired. Amie Potter machine-outline-quilted the appliqués, stitched loops in the sashing strip backgrounds, and added feathered cable motifs in the border (**Quilting Diagram**).

**5** Referring to Complete Quilt, join green print bias binding strips into one long strip. Cut one end of strip diagonally and fold under; this will be the starting end. Fold strip in half lengthwise with wrong sides together; press. Beginning at top of a scallop, align the long raw edges of the bias strip with the marked line.

**QUILTING DIAGRAM**

Beginning about 2" from folded starting end, sew through all layers with ¼" seam allowance, stopping at point of first V between two scallops. With needle down, lift presser foot. Pivot layers to stitch binding to next scallop. The binding will be pulled tightly around the V, so be careful not to sew in any folds or pleats. Sew around quilt, ending with a small diagonal overlap of binding at folded end. Carefully trim all layers on marked line.

Fold binding edge to back, covering stitching. Hand-stitch binding to backing fabric. To make miters at each V, hand-stitch up to V and work inside corners to create a small pleat on each side. Take a stitch or two to secure it. Then stitch binding in place up to the next V.

# COLOR OPTION

Opulent fabrics and stately rows of Flying Geese units set apart quilt tester Laura Boehnke's version of *Fly into Spring*. Choose a bold, tapestry-like floral for the 8"-wide sashing to achieve a similar effect.

# mini
# make-do

INSPIRED BY **NATURE'S NEUTRALS**
FROM DESIGNER **DEBRA L. ROBERTS**
**OF THE QUILTED MOOSE**
(quiltedmooseonline.com)

Like shortcuts?
A charm pack is perfect
for this scrappy table topper's
2½" squares and narrow strips.

## materials

- 40 to 60—5" precut squares *or* 1⅜ yards total assorted prints in red, pink, white, black, yellow, blue, green, and purple
- ⅓ yard blue polka dot (binding)
- ¾ yard backing fabric
- 27×31" batting

Finished quilt: 18½×23"
Finished block: 4½" square

Quantities are for precut 5" squares and 44/45"-wide, 100% cotton fabrics. Measurements include ¼" seam allowances. Sew with right sides together unless otherwise stated.

## select fabrics

Use the total yardage listed as a guide when choosing assorted fabrics from your stash.

To get the scrappy look she wanted, quiltmaker Laura Boehnke used 52 precut charm (5") squares in this small table topper. For the scrappiest look possible, use 60 charm squares in assorted prints.

To conserve fabric, use a minimum of 40 charm squares in assorted prints.

## cut fabrics

Cut pieces in the following order.

Pinked edges are included in measurements in **Cutting Diagrams A** and **B**. Before cutting, be sure to measure 5" squares from the outermost points of the pinked edges to see if the points are included in the stated size.

If using 60 charm squares in assorted prints, cut a set of two 1¼×5" strips and two 1¼×3½" strips from each of 20 charm squares (**Cutting Diagram A**). Then cut a set of two 1×3½" strips and two 1×2½" strips from each of 20 remaining charm squares, and one 2½" square from each remaining charm square.

**CUTTING DIAGRAM A**

If using 40 charm squares in assorted prints, cut a set of two 1¼×5" strips and two 1¼×3½" strips from each of 20 charm squares (**Cutting Diagram A**). Referring to **Cutting Diagram B**, cut a set of two 1×3½" strips, two 1×2½" strips, and a 2½" square from each of the remaining charm squares.

**CUTTING DIAGRAM B**

**From assorted prints, cut:**
- 20 sets of 2 matching 1¼×5" strips and 2 matching 1¼×3½" strips
- 20 sets of 2 matching 1×3½" strips and 2 matching 1×2½" strips
- 20—2½" squares

**From blue polka dot, cut:**
- 3—2½×42" binding strips

*To tame loosely woven fabrics or ensure stripes and plaids stay on grain, spray them with starch or sizing and press well before cutting and piecing.*

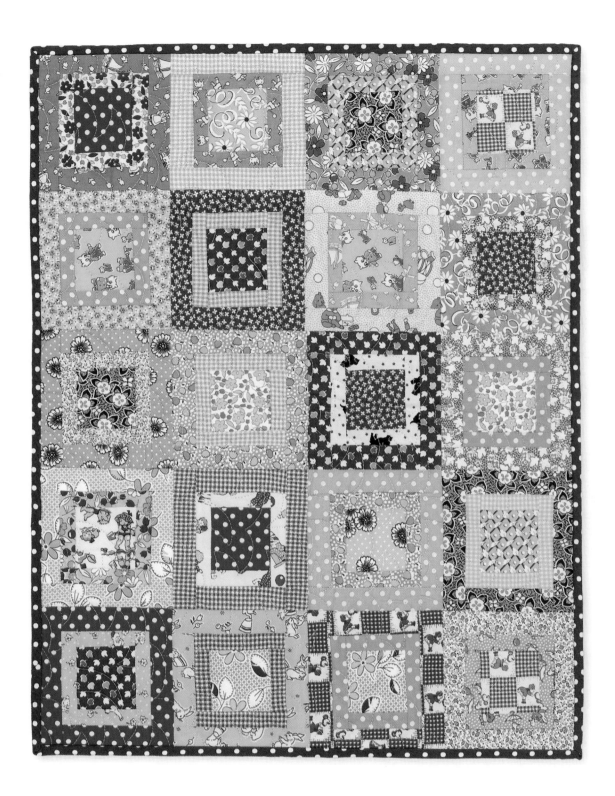

QUILT ASSEMBLY DIAGRAM

*When selecting fabrics, use a color wheel to help make
pleasing color combinations. This handy tool makes color relationships
easy to see by dividing the spectrum in 12 basic hues.*

## assemble blocks

**1** For one block, gather two 1×3½" strips and two 1×2½" strips from one print, two 1¼×5" strips and two 1¼×3½" strips from a second print, and one 2½" square from a third print.

**2** Sew assorted print 1×2½" strips to opposite edges of assorted print 2½" square **(Diagram 1)**. Press seams toward strips. Add assorted print 1×3½" strips to remaining edges to make block center. Press seams toward strips.

**DIAGRAM 1**

**3** Join assorted print 1¼×3½" strips to opposite edges of block center **(Diagram 2)**. Add assorted print 1¼×5" strips to remaining edges to make a block. Press all seams away from block center. The block should be 5" square including seam allowances.

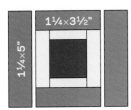

**DIAGRAM 2**

**4** Repeat steps 1–3 to make 20 blocks total.

## assemble quilt top

**1** Referring to Quilt Assembly Diagram, lay out blocks in five rows, rotating every other block to alternate block seams.

**2** Sew together blocks in each row. Press seams in one direction, alternating direction with each row. Join rows to complete quilt top. Press seams in one direction.

## finish quilt

**1** Layer quilt top, batting, and backing; baste. (For details, see Complete Quilt, *page 175*.)

**2** Quilt as desired. Machine-quilter Nancy Sharr stitched a stylized feather motif across the quilt top.

**3** Bind with blue polka dot binding strips. (For details, see Complete Quilt.)

It's easier than it looks!
Raw-edge triangles stitched
atop a square create the
dramatic X in each block.

# ROUGH
## AROUND THE EDGES

DESIGNER **LYNNE HAGMEIER OF
KANSAS TROUBLES QUILTERS** (ktquilts.com)

## materials

- 35—10" precut squares in assorted light, medium, and dark prints (blocks)
- 70—5" precut squares in assorted light, medium, and dark prints (appliqués)
- ⅔ yard tan print (inner border)
- 2⅛ yards green print (outer border, binding)
- 5⅛ yards backing fabric
- 72×91" batting
- Pinking shears or rotary cutter with pinking blade

Finished quilt: 64×83"
Finished block: 9½" square

Quantities are for precut 10" and 5" squares and 44/45"-wide, 100% cotton fabrics.
Measurements include ¼" seam allowances. Sew with right sides together unless otherwise stated.

## cut fabrics

Cut pieces in the following order.

To plan this quilt in your own colorway, use the **Coloring Diagram** on *Pattern Sheet 2*.

If you prefer to use light, medium, and dark print yardages instead of 10" and 5" precut squares, you will need 35—18×22" pieces (fat quarters). From each fat quarter, cut 1—10" square and 2—5" squares.

**From tan print, cut:**
- 7—2½×42" strips for inner border

**From green print, cut:**
- 7—6½×42" strips for outer border
- 8—2½×42" binding strips

## appliqué blocks

1 Referring to **Diagram 1**, if edges of precut squares are not already pinked, use pinking shears to pink all edges of an assorted light, medium, or dark print 5" square (see tip, *page 138*). Using straight-blade fabric scissors or a rotary cutter, cut square in half diagonally to make two pinked triangles. Repeat to make 140 pinked triangles total.

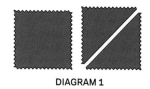

DIAGRAM 1

2 Fold an assorted light, medium, or dark print 10" square in half horizontally and vertically. Finger-press folds lightly to make a foundation square with placement guidelines; unfold square **(Diagram 2)**.

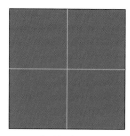

DIAGRAM 2

3 Select four assorted pinked triangles that contrast with foundation square. Fold a triangle in half widthwise; finger-press fold lightly to make a triangle with a placement guideline **(Diagram 3)**. Repeat to make four triangles with placement guidelines total.

DIAGRAM 3

4 Referring to **Diagram 4**, lay a prepared foundation square right side up on flat surface. Lay a triangle with a placement guideline right side up along one edge of square, aligning edges and matching placement guidelines.

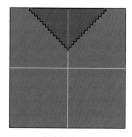

DIAGRAM 4

Pin pieces together. With matching thread, machine-straight-stitch ⅛" from pinked edges of triangle. Repeat to stitch remaining triangles with placement guidelines on remaining edges of square to make an appliquéd block **(Diagram 5)**. The block should be 10" square including seam allowances.

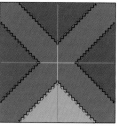

DIAGRAM 5

5 Repeat steps 2–4 to make 35 appliquéd blocks total.

## assemble quilt center

**1** Referring to Quilt Assembly Diagram, lay out blocks in seven horizontal rows.

**2** Sew together blocks in each row. Press seams in one direction, alternating direction with each row.

**3** Join rows to make quilt center. Press seams in one direction. The quilt center should be 48×67" including seam allowances.

## add borders

**1** Cut and piece tan print 2½×42" strips to make:
- 2—2½×67" inner border strips
- 2—2½×52" inner border strips

**2** Sew long inner border strips to long edges of quilt center. Add short inner border strips to remaining edges. Press all seams toward inner border.

**3** Cut and piece green print 6½×42" strips to make:
- 2—6½×71" outer border strips
- 2—6½×64" outer border strips

**4** Sew long outer border strips to long edges of quilt center. Add short outer border strips to remaining edges to complete quilt top. Press all seams toward outer border.

## finish quilt

**1** Layer quilt top, batting, and backing; baste. (For details, see Complete Quilt, *page 175.*)

**2** Quilt as desired. Kristi's Quilt Farm stitched in the ditch around the blocks and borders. The quilter stitched Xs in the block foundations and sets of parallel lines 2" apart in the inner border. Feather motifs accent the triangle appliqués and outer border.

**3** Bind with green print binding strips. (For details, see Complete Quilt.)

*Pinking shears—scissors with edges that cut a zigzag pattern—create texture on the short edges of each triangle and give the quilt a casual, folk art look. If the quilt is washed, the pinked edges will take on a more feathery appearance. A rotary-cutter pinking blade also can be used to pink the triangles. Both pinking shears and blades are available at quilting or crafts supply stores.*

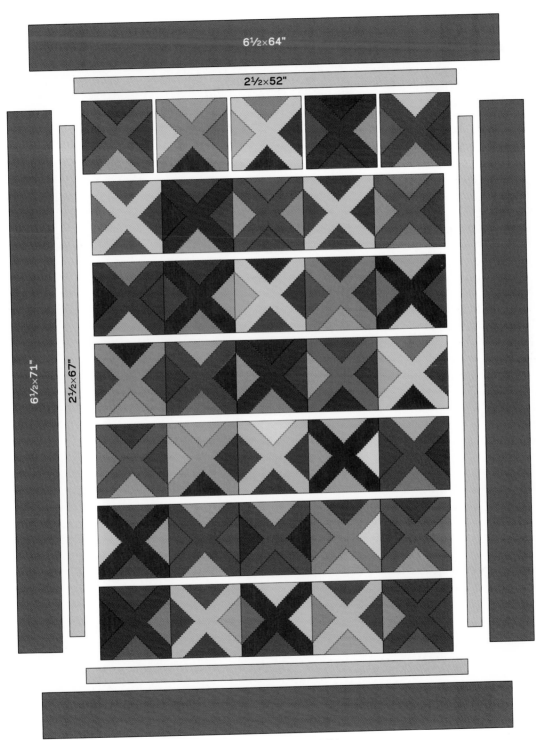

QUILT ASSEMBLY DIAGRAM

# bay*breeze*

The recipe for this table mat is simple: Just mix together a batch of charm squares with two fat quarters.

DESIGNER **MONICA SOLORIO-SNOW OF HAPPY ZOMBIE** (thehappyzombie.com)

## materials

- 16—5" precut squares in assorted medium and dark prints (blocks, border)
- 3—5" squares in assorted ecru florals (setting squares)
- 6—5" squares in assorted pink prints (setting and corner triangles)
- 18×22" piece (fat quarter) green print (piping, binding)
- 18×22" piece (fat quarter) backing fabric
- 18×22" batting

**Finished quilt:** 14½×17"
**Finished block:** 2" square

**Quantities** are for precut 5" squares and 44/45"-wide, 100% cotton fabrics. **Measurements** include ¼" seam allowances. Sew with right sides together unless otherwise stated.

## about the fabrics

Designer Monica Solorio-Snow enjoys using 5"-square charm packs to make quick weekend projects, such as this mini quilt. Purchase a charm pack of 5" squares as she did, or select coordinating prints from your stash. To make the Four-Patch blocks more prominent, choose high-contrast and/or small-scale prints.

Monica suggests using the little quilt to dress up a tabletop or an antique doll bed, or grouping several of the quilts as a wall arrangement. "Start to finish, it's big fun in a little quilt," she says.

## cut fabrics

Cut pieces in the following order.

**From assorted medium and dark prints, cut:**
- 8—$1\frac{1}{2}$×$1\frac{5}{8}$" rectangles
- 128—$1\frac{1}{2}$" squares

**From assorted ecru florals, cut:**
- 12—$2\frac{1}{2}$" setting squares

**From assorted pink prints, cut:**
- 4—$4\frac{3}{4}$" squares, cutting each diagonally twice in an X for 16 setting triangles total (you will use 14)
- 2—3" squares, cutting each in half diagonally for 4 corner triangles total

**From green print, cut:**
- 4—$2\frac{1}{2}$×22" binding strips
- 2—$\frac{3}{4}$×15" piping strips
- 2—$\frac{3}{4}$×$12\frac{1}{2}$" piping strips

## assemble blocks

Sew together four assorted medium and dark print $1\frac{1}{2}$" squares in pairs (**Diagram 1**). Press seams in opposite directions. Join pairs to make a Four-Patch block; press seam in one direction. The block should be $2\frac{1}{2}$" square including seam allowances. Repeat to make 20 Four-Patch blocks total.

DIAGRAM 1

## assemble quilt center

1 Referring to photo, *opposite*, lay out Four-Patch blocks, assorted ecru floral setting squares, and assorted pink print setting triangles in diagonal rows.

2 Sew together pieces in each row. Press seams toward setting squares and triangles. Join rows; press seams in one direction. Add assorted pink print corner triangles to make quilt center; press seams toward corner triangles.

3 Referring to **Diagram 2**, trim quilt center to $12\frac{1}{2}$×15" including seam allowances (leave at least $\frac{1}{2}$" beyond outside corner of each Four-Patch block on long edges).

## add piping

1 With wrong side inside, fold each green print $\frac{3}{4}$×$12\frac{1}{2}$" piping strip in half lengthwise; press. Repeat with $\frac{3}{4}$×15" piping strips.

2 Aligning raw edges, baste short piping strips to short edges of quilt center using a scant $\frac{1}{4}$" seam allowance. Baste long piping strips to remaining edges. The quilt center should still be $12\frac{1}{2}$×15" including seam allowances.

DIAGRAM 2

## add border

1 Sew together 10 assorted medium and dark print 1½" squares and four 1½×1⅝" rectangles to make a long border strip. Press seams in one direction. The long border strip should be 1½×15" including seam allowances. Repeat to make a second long border strip.

2 Sew together 14 assorted medium and dark print 1½" squares to make a short border strip. Press seams in one direction. The short border strip should be 1½×14½" including seam allowances. Repeat to make a second short border strip.

3 Sew long border strips to long edges of quilt center. Join short border strips to remaining edges to complete quilt top. Press all seams toward border.

## finish quilt

1 Layer quilt top, batting, and backing; baste. (For details, see Complete Quilt, *page 175*.)

2 Quilt as desired. Monica hand-outline-quilted ¼" inside each setting square and triangle and stitched in the ditch around the Four-Patch blocks.

3 Bind with green print binding strips. (For details, see Complete Quilt.)

*The piping on this quilt does not contain a cord. It's simply a folded flap of fabric that adds a dash of interest.*

Start—and finish—this quilt today without any muss or fuss. It's a great first project or a perfect way for quilters to use their stash.

DESIGNER **ANNA SITAR OF LAUNDRY BASKET QUILTS**
(laundrybasketquilts.com)

# sew easy

## materials

- 36—10" precut squares in assorted prints, florals, stripes, and dots in rose, aqua, orange, and green (squares)
- 1¼ yards green tone-on-tone (border)
- ⅝ yard pink print (binding)
- 4⅓ yards backing fabric
- 77" square batting

Finished quilt: 68½" square

**Quantities** are for precut 10" squares and 44/45"-wide, 100% cotton fabrics.
**Measurements** include ¼" seam allowances. Sew with right sides together unless otherwise stated.

## select fabrics

Purchase a precut bundle of 10" squares to eliminate cutting the squares yourself and give your quilt a sampling of an entire fabric collection.

If you pull fabrics from your personal stash and the collection leans toward one value, either light or dark, trade 10" squares with quilting friends. By swapping 10" squares, you'll expand your stash—and theirs—without adding large fabric pieces in colors you don't often use.

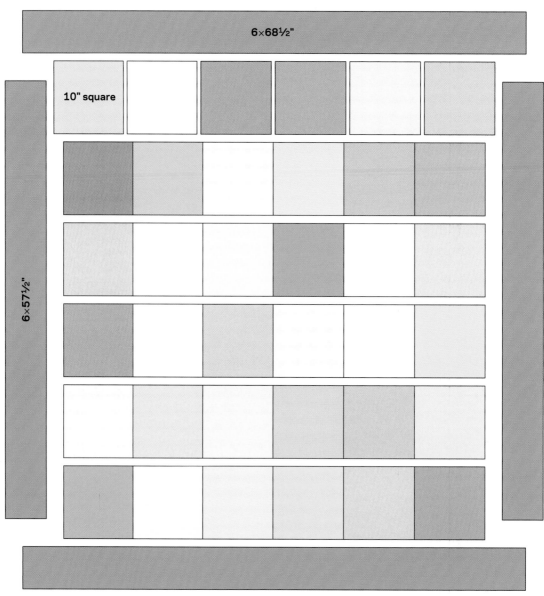

6×68½"

10" square

6×57½"

**QUILT ASSEMBLY DIAGRAM**

## cut fabrics

Cut fabrics in the following order.

**From green tone-on-tone, cut:**
- 7—6×42" strips for border

**From pink print, cut:**
- 7—2½×42" binding strips

## assemble quilt center

1 Referring to **Quilt Assembly Diagram,** lay out assorted print, floral, stripe, and dot 10" squares in six horizontal rows.

2 Sew together squares in each row. Press seams in one direction, alternating direction with each row.

3 Join rows to make quilt center. Press seams in one direction. The quilt center should be 57½" square including seam allowances.

## add border

1 Cut and piece green tone-on-tone 6×42" strips to make:
- 2—6×68½" border strips
- 2—6×57½" border strips

2 Sew short border strips to opposite edges of quilt center (**Quilt Assembly Diagram**). Add long border strips to remaining edges to complete quilt top. Press all seams toward border.

## finish quilt

1 Layer quilt top, batting, and backing; baste. (For details, see Complete Quilt, *page 175*.)

2 Quilt as desired. Designer Anna Sitar machine-quilted an allover feather design across the quilt top.

3 Bind with pink print binding strips. (For details, see Complete Quilt.)

# Finishing Tips

### EASIEST MACHINE-QUILTING EVER

Stitch parallel diagonal lines in a grid (**Quilting Diagram**). Use chalk or a water-soluble marker to mark the lines before beginning to stitch. Using a walking (even-feed) foot, first stitch the center (longest) lines in both directions, then work toward the outer edges.

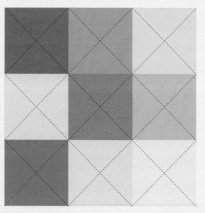

**QUILTING DIAGRAM**

### FASTEST FINISH EVER

Tying a quilt is a quick alternative to machine quilting. Choose a suitable batting, because there will be large unquilted areas between ties.

Use a large-eye needle and six-ply embroidery floss or perle cotton for ties. Make a single running stitch through all quilt layers, beginning and ending on the quilt top and leaving a 3" tail (**Photo A**). Make a single backstitch through the same holes and all three layers, ending on the quilt top (**Photo B**). Clip thread, leaving a second 3" tail (**Photo C**). Tie tails in a square knot (right over left, then left over right) close to the quilt surface (**Photo D**). Avoid pulling too tight and puckering the fabric. Clip thread tails as short as desired.

## COLOR OPTION

Mix it up! Buy a bundle of precut squares, or cut a variety of squares from your stash. spread them out the floor or on a design wall, and the surprises beg Play around with arrangement—ta some out, try a different color, fli over, or rotate str so they all run the same direction (o opposing directio You'll be amazed the patterns that emerge—dramati designs, colors th pop, and subtle movements. Che out this sampling some eye-catchin possibilities.

...antic pastels and neutrals softly surround one bright ...square that gives this throw a punch of color.

High contrast between squares makes this winter collection sparkle, yet the scrappy Nine-Patch setting allows the darker blocks to recede.

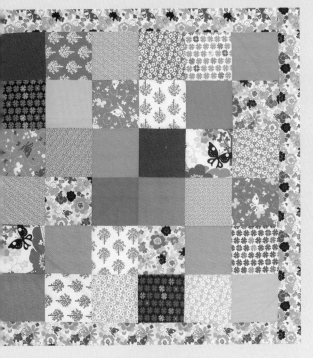

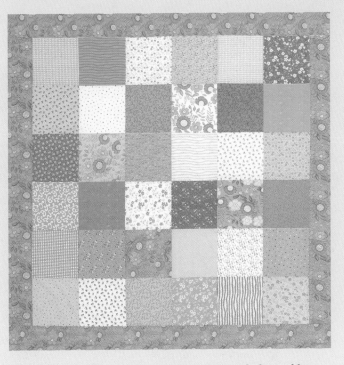

...solid squares form a Four-Patch center and extend ...onally to all corners, giving the eye places to rest amid ...usy prints.

A warm spring-into-summer color palette is balanced by careful placement of the cooler blue and white squares sprinkled across this scrappy design.

A scrappy assortment of signature blocks makes a heartwarming keepsake throw to keep or give as a gift.

DESIGNER **JO MORTON**
(jomortonquilts.com)

# *friendship* ALBUM

## materials

- 42—10" precut squares* *or* 3 yards total assorted prints in green, brown, gold, rust, blue, and black (blocks)
  *One 10" square will yield enough pieces for one block (see **Cutting Diagram,** *page 152*)
- ⅞ yard solid cream (blocks)
- 2 yards cream print (blocks)
- 1⅞ yards rust print (sashing)
- ⅞ yard gold print (sashing squares, binding)
- 5 yards backing fabric
- 77×88" batting
- Fine-point permanent marking pen: brown or black (optional)

Finished quilt: 68¼×79¼"
Finished block: 9¼" square

Quantities are for precut 10" squares and 44/45"-wide, 100% cotton fabrics.
Measurements include ¼" seam allowances. Sew with right sides together unless otherwise stated.

 **SIZE OPTIONS:** For a chart of optional sizes, turn to *Pattern Sheet 2.*

## cut fabrics

Cut pieces in the following order.

To plan this quilt in your own colorway, use the **Coloring Diagram** on *Pattern Sheet 2*.

**From *each* assorted print 10" square, refer to Cutting Diagram and cut:**

- 2—2⅛×5⅜" rectangles
- 6—2⅛×3¾" rectangles
- 2—2⅛" squares

**From solid cream, cut:**

- 42—2⅛×5⅜" rectangles
- 84—2⅛" squares

**From cream print, cut:**

- 126—4" squares, cutting each diagonally twice in an X for 504 large triangles total
- 84—2½" squares, cutting each in half diagonally for 168 small triangles total

**From rust print, cut:**

- 97—2¼×9¾" sashing rectangles

**From gold print, cut:**

- 8—2½×42" binding strips
- 56—2¼" sashing squares

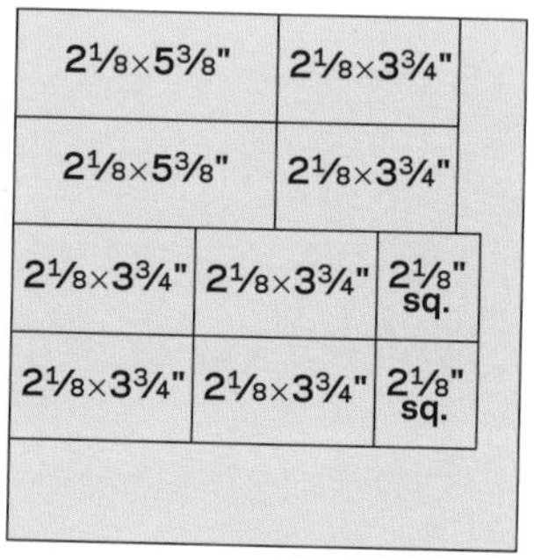

| | |
|---|---|
| 2⅛×5⅜" | 2⅛×3¾" |
| 2⅛×5⅜" | 2⅛×3¾" |

| | | |
|---|---|---|
| 2⅛×3¾" | 2⅛×3¾" | 2⅛" sq. |
| 2⅛×3¾" | 2⅛×3¾" | 2⅛" sq. |

**CUTTING DIAGRAM**

## assemble blocks

**1** For one Chimney Sweep block, gather one set of matching print pieces (two 2⅛×5⅜" rectangles, six 2⅛×3¾" rectangles, and two 2⅛" squares), one solid cream 2⅛×5⅜" rectangle, two solid cream 2⅛" squares, 12 cream print large triangles, and four cream print small triangles.

**2** Referring to **Diagram 1**, lay out all pieces except small triangles in rows. Sew together pieces in each row. Press seams toward assorted print squares and rectangles. Join rows; press seams in one direction.

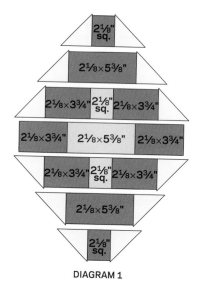

**DIAGRAM 1**

**3** Add a cream print small triangle to each corner to make a Chimney Sweep block (Diagram 2). Press seams away from corners. Trim block to 9¾" square including seam allowances.

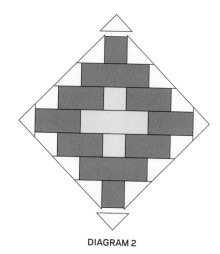

**DIAGRAM 2**

**4** Repeat steps 1–3 to make 42 Chimney Sweep blocks total.

## assemble quilt top

**1** Referring to **Quilt Assembly Diagram**, lay out blocks, rust print sashing rectangles, and gold print sashing squares in 15 horizontal rows. Sew together pieces in each row. Press seams toward sashing rectangles.

**2** Join rows to complete quilt top. Press seams toward sashing rows.

**3** If desired, add signatures to solid cream block centers, *page 155*, using a fine-point permanent marking pen.

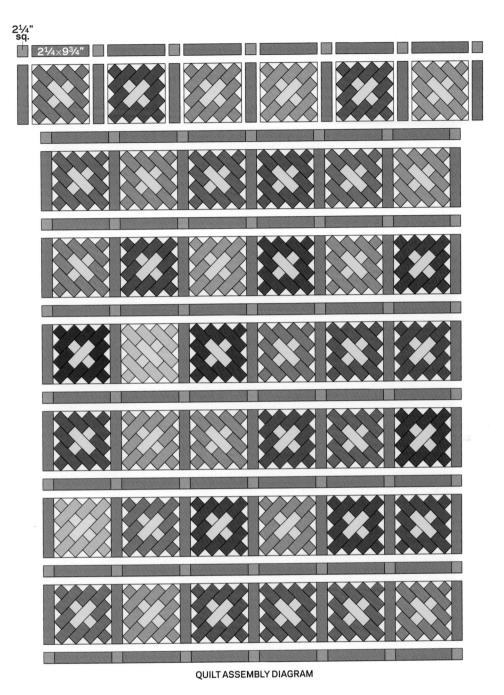

**2¼" sq.**

**2¼×9¾"**

**QUILT ASSEMBLY DIAGRAM**

*"For years I have turned to antique quilts as an inspiration source for color and design. I like low-contrast quilts, as they usually look old and worn. Among my favorites are quilts with brown in them— they have a warm, comfortable charm."*

—DESIGNER JO MORTON

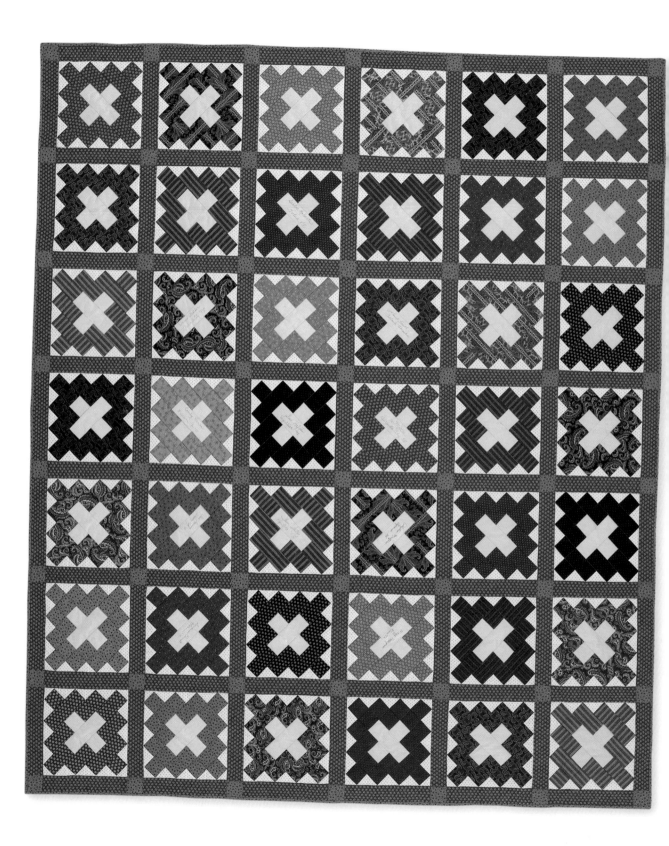

## finish quilt

1 Layer quilt top, batting, and backing; baste. (For details, see Complete Quilt, *page 175*.)

2 Quilt as desired. Maggi Honeyman machine-quilted in the ditch in the blocks and stitched a vine design in the sashing rectangles (Quilting Diagram).

**QUILTING DIAGRAM**

3 Bind with gold print binding strips. (For details, see Complete Quilt.)

## COLOR OPTION

For this playful kid's version of *Friendship Album*, quilt tester Laura Boehnke reined in a variety of colorful, contrasting blocks with a bold tone-on-tone sashing. Use the 35¼×46¼" quilt as a table cover at a child's birthday party and create a memorable keepsake by having partygoers and family members sign the block centers.

*To sign blocks, use a fine-point permanent marking pen, then heat-set for two minutes using a hot, dry iron.*

# so
# charming

Choose your favorite charm pack of assorted precut 5" squares, add in ½ yard of solid cream, then take your pick of these fast and fun projects.

DESIGNERS (PILLOW) **MONICA SOLORIO-SNOW OF HAPPY ZOMBIE** (thehappyzombie.com), (POT HOLDERS) **CAMILLE ROSKELLEY OF THIMBLE BLOSSOMS** (camilleroskelley.typepad.com), and (TABLE TOPPER) **JOANNA FIGUEROA OF FIG TREE & CO.** (figtreequilts.com)

## cut fabrics

Cut pieces in the following order.

**From *each* of 16 assorted print, solid, or stripe 5" squares, cut:**
- 1—1½×3½" rectangle
- 2—1½" squares

**From *each* of 5 remaining assorted print, solid, or stripe 5" squares, cut:**
- 4—1½" squares

**From solid cream, cut:**
- 2—16½"×20½" rectangles
- 44—1½" squares

**From *each* assorted tan and cream print 5" square, cut:**
- 1—3½" setting square

**From *each* assorted blue print 5" square, cut:**
- 1—4⅞" square, cutting each in half diagonally for 16 setting and corner triangles total

## assemble blocks

**1** Lay out one 1½×3½" rectangle and two 1½" squares from one print, solid, or stripe and four solid cream 1½" squares in three horizontal rows **(Diagram 1)**.

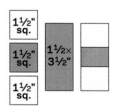

**DIAGRAM 1**

**2** Sew together squares in each pieced row. Press seams toward center square.

## materials *for the pillow*

- 21—5"-square assorted prints, solids, and stripes in green, red, yellow, and light blue (blocks)
- ⅔ yard solid cream (blocks, pillow back)
- 9—5"-square assorted prints in tan and cream (setting squares)
- 8—5" squares in assorted blue prints (setting and corner triangles)
- 20" square muslin
- 20" square batting
- 16"-square pillow form

**Finished pillow:** 16" square
**Finished block:** 3" square

**Quantities** are for 44/45"-wide, 100% cotton fabrics.
**Measurements** include ¼" seam allowances. Sew with right sides together unless otherwise stated.

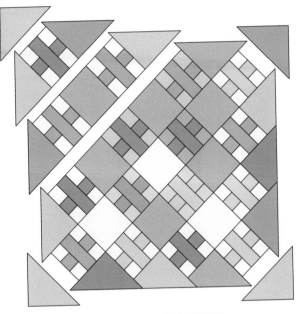

PILLOW TOP ASSEMBLY DIAGRAM

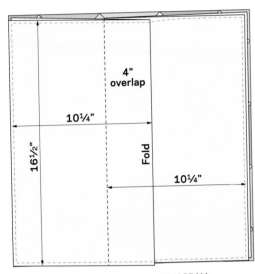

PILLOW BACK ASSEMBLY DIAGRAM

**3** Join rows to make a block (**Diagram 2**). Press seams toward center rectangle. Block should be 3½" square including seam allowances.

DIAGRAM 2

**4** Repeat steps 1–3 to make 16 blocks total.

## assemble and quilt pillow top

**1** Referring to **Pillow Top Assembly Diagram,** lay out blocks, setting squares, and setting triangles in seven diagonal rows.

**2** Sew together pieces in each row, being careful not to stretch bias edges of triangles. Press seams toward setting squares and triangles.

**3** Add corner triangles, again being careful not to stretch bias edges, to make pillow top. Press seams toward triangles.

**4** Trim pillow top to 16½" square.

**5** Layer pillow top, batting, and muslin; baste. Quilt as desired. Trim batting and lining even with pillow top edges.

## finish pillow

**1** With wrong sides inside, fold two solid cream 16½×20½" rectangles in half to form two double-thick 10¼×16½" rectangles. (The double thickness makes the pillow back more stable.) Overlap folded edges by about 4" to make a 16½" square (**Pillow Back Assembly Diagram**). Baste around square to make pillow back.

**2** With right sides together, layer quilted pillow top with pillow back; pin. Sew together around outer edges. Turn right side out. Insert pillow form through opening to complete pillow.

## assemble pot holders

1 Referring to **Diagram 1**, lay out 20 assorted floral, print, and stripe 2½" squares in four rows. Sew together squares in each row. Press seams open. Join rows to make a front unit. Press seams open. The front unit should be 10½×8½" including seam allowances.

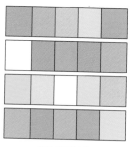

**DIAGRAM 1**

2 Center front unit right side up atop insulated batting, cotton batting, and muslin 9×11" rectangles; baste. (For details, see Complete Quilt, *page 175*.)

3 Quilt as desired. Designer Camille Roskelley machine-quilted a loop pattern across the front unit.

4 Trim batting and muslin even with front unit to make quilted pocket rectangle. The pocket rectangle should be 10½×8½" including seam allowances.

### materials *for two pot holders*

- 23—5" squares or ¾ yard total assorted florals, prints, and stripes in blue, tan, yellow, coral, cream, green, and aqua (squares)
- ½ yard solid cream (binding)
- ⅜ yard muslin (backing)
- 24" square each of cotton batting and insulated batting, such as Insul-Bright (warmcompany.com)

Finished pot holder: 10½" square

Quantities are for 44/45"-wide, 100% cotton fabrics. Measurements include ¼" seam allowances. Sew with right sides together unless otherwise stated.

## cut fabrics

Cut pieces in the following order.

Corner Cutting Pattern is on *Pattern Sheet 1*. To make a template of the pattern, see Make and Use Templates, *page 171*.

**From 23 assorted floral, print, and stripe 5" squares, refer to Cutting Diagram 2 on *page 163* and cut:**

- 90—2½" squares

**From solid cream, cut:**

- Enough 2½"-wide bias strips to total 120", cutting and piecing to make 2—2½×44" and 2—2½×10½" binding strips (For details, see Cut Bias Strips, *page 170*.)

**From muslin, cut:**

- 2—11" squares
- 2—9×11" rectangles

**From each cotton and insulated batting, cut:**

- 2—11" squares
- 2—9×11" rectangles

**5** Using Corner Cutting Pattern on *Pattern Sheet 1*, mark cutting line at corners of one long edge of pocket rectangle for rounding corners **(Diagram 2)**. Machine-baste a scant ⅛" inside lines. Trim along marked lines. Machine-baste remaining edges.

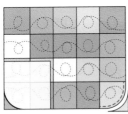

DIAGRAM 2

**6** Using one solid cream 2½×10½" bias strip, bind straight edge of pocket rectangle. (For details, see Complete Quilt, *page 175*.)

**7** Lay out 25 assorted floral, print, and stripe 2½" squares in five rows **(Diagram 3)**. Sew together squares in each row. Press seams open. Join rows to make a back unit. Press seams open. The back unit should be 10½" square including seam allowances.

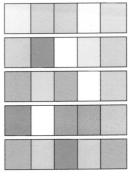

DIAGRAM 3

**8** Center back unit right side up atop insulated batting, cotton batting, and muslin 11" squares; baste as before.

**9** Quilt as desired. Camille machine-quilted a scallop pattern across the back unit.

**10** Trim batting and muslin even with back unit to make quilted back piece. The back piece should be 10½" square including seam allowances. Using Corner Cutting Pattern on *Pattern Sheet 1*, and referring to Step 5, mark, stitch, and trim all corners on back piece. Machine-baste around all edges as before.

**11** With right sides facing up, layer pocket rectangle atop back piece. Join together using ⅛" seam **(Diagram 4)**.

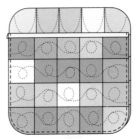

DIAGRAM 4

**12** Using a solid cream 2½×44" bias strip, bind outer edges to complete one pot holder.

**13** Repeat steps 1–12 to make a second pot holder.

> **"*Making projects for my home and family is one of my favorite things to do.*"**
> —CAMILLE ROSKELLEY

## cut fabrics

Cut pieces in the following order.

**From cream floral 5" square, cut:**
- 1—4½" square

**From 13 assorted floral, print, and stripe 5" squares, refer to Cutting Diagram 1 and cut:**
- 26—2½×5" rectangles

**From remaining assorted floral, print, and stripe 5" squares, refer to Cutting Diagram 2 and cut:**
- 84—2½" squares

**From solid cream, refer to Cutting Diagram 3 and cut:**
- 4—2½×24½" border No. 5 strips
- 4—2½×16½" border No. 3 strips
- 2—2½×12½" border No. 1 strips
- 2—2½×8½" border No. 1 strips
- 12—2½×4½" rectangles
- 8—2½" squares

### materials *for the table topper*
- 5" square cream floral (center unit)
- 34—5" squares or 1¼ yards total assorted florals, prints, and stripes in cream, coral, blue, green, yellow, tan, and aqua (center unit, borders, binding)
- ½ yard solid cream (borders)
- 36" square backing fabric
- 36" square batting

Finished table topper: 28½" square

**Quantities** are for 44/45"-wide, 100% cotton fabrics. **Measurements** include ¼" seam allowances. Sew with right sides together unless otherwise stated.

## assemble center unit

**1** Referring to **Diagram 1**, join two assorted floral, print, or stripe 2½" squares in a pair. Press seam in one direction. Repeat to make a second pair.

**DIAGRAM 1**

**2** Referring to **Diagram 2**, sew pairs to opposite edges of cream floral 4½" square. Press seams toward pairs.

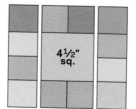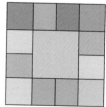

**DIAGRAM 2**

**CUTTING DIAGRAM 1**

$2\frac{1}{2} \times 5$" | $2\frac{1}{2} \times 5$"

**CUTTING DIAGRAM 2**

$2\frac{1}{2}$" sq. | $2\frac{1}{2}$" sq.
$2\frac{1}{2}$" sq. | $2\frac{1}{2}$" sq.

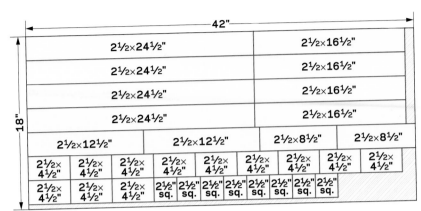

**CUTTING DIAGRAM 3**

| 42" | | 18" |
|---|---|---|

3. Join four assorted floral, print, or stripe $2\frac{1}{2}$" squares to make a row. Press seams in one direction. Repeat to make a second row.

4. Add rows to remaining edges of cream floral $4\frac{1}{2}$" square to make center unit (Diagram 2). Press seams toward rows. The center unit should be $8\frac{1}{2}$" square including seam allowances.

## add border no. 1

Referring to **Table Topper Assembly Diagram,** sew solid cream $2\frac{1}{2} \times 8\frac{1}{2}$" border No. 1 strips to opposite edges of center unit. Add solid cream $2\frac{1}{2} \times 12\frac{1}{2}$" border No. 1 strips to remaining edges. Press all seams toward border.

## assemble and add border no. 2

1. Use a pencil to mark a diagonal line on wrong side of 24 assorted floral, print, and stripe $2\frac{1}{2}$" squares. (To prevent fabric from stretching as you draw lines, place 220-grit sandpaper under each square.)

2. Align a marked floral, print, or stripe square with one end of a solid cream $2\frac{1}{2} \times 4\frac{1}{2}$" rectangle (Diagram 3; note direction of drawn line). Stitch on marked line, then trim excess, leaving a $\frac{1}{4}$" seam allowance. Press open attached triangle.

3. Align a second marked floral, print, or stripe square with opposite end of Step 2

**DIAGRAM 3**

rectangle (Diagram 3; note direction of drawn line). Stitch, trim, and press as before to make a Flying Geese unit. The Flying Geese unit should be $4\frac{1}{2} \times 2\frac{1}{2}$" including seam allowances.

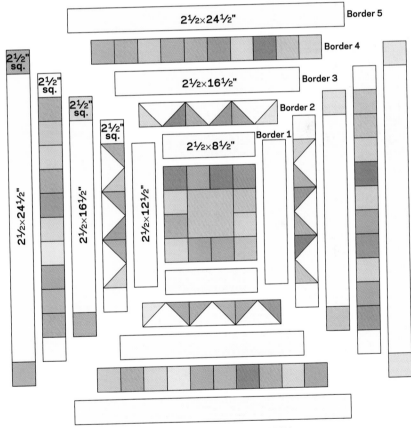

**TABLE TOPPER ASSEMBLY DIAGRAM**

**4** Repeat steps 2 and 3 to make 12 Flying Geese units total.

**5** Referring to **Table Topper Assembly Diagram,** *page 163,* sew together three Flying Geese units in a row to make a short border No. 2 strip. Press seams in one direction. The strip should be 2½×12½" including seam allowances. Repeat to make a second short border No. 2 strip. Add short border No. 2 strips to opposite edges of center unit. Press seams toward border No. 2.

**6** Join two solid cream 2½" squares and three Flying Geese units to make a long border No. 2 strip (**Table Topper Assembly Diagram**). Press seams toward Flying Geese units. The strip should be 2½×16½" including seam allowances. Repeat to make a second long border No. 2 strip. Add long border No. 2 strips to remaining edges of center unit. Press seams toward border No. 2.

## add border nos. 3, 4, and 5

**1** Sew two solid cream 2½×16½" border No. 3 strips to opposite edges of center unit. Press seams toward border No. 3.

**2** Join two assorted floral, print, or stripe 2½" squares to opposite ends of a solid cream 2½×16½" strip to make a long border No. 3 strip (**Table Topper Assembly Diagram on** *page 163*). Press seams toward solid cream. The strip should be 2½×20½" including seam allowances. Repeat to make a second long border No. 3 strip.

**3** Join long border No. 3 strips to remaining edges of center unit. Press seams toward border No. 3.

**4** Referring to **Table Topper Assembly Diagram,** sew together 10 assorted floral, print, and stripe 2½" squares to make a short border No. 4 strip. Press seams in one direction. The strip should be 2½×20½" including seam allowances. Repeat to make a second short border No. 4 strip. Join short border No. 4 strips to opposite edges of center unit. Press seams toward border No. 4.

**5** Sew together two solid cream 2½" squares and 10 assorted floral, print, and stripe 2½" squares to make a long border No. 4 strip (**Table Topper Assembly Diagram**). Press seams in one direction. The strip should be 2½×24½" including seam allowances. Repeat to make a second long border No. 4 strip. Add long border No. 4 strips to remaining edges of center unit. Press seams toward border No. 4.

**6** Sew solid cream 2½×24½" border No. 5 strips to opposite edges of center unit. Press seams toward border No. 5.

**7** Join two assorted floral, print, or stripe 2½" squares to ends of a solid cream 2½×24½" strip to make a long border No. 5 strip. Press seams toward solid cream strip. Repeat to make a second long border No. 5 strip. The strip should be 2½×28½" including seam allowances. Join long border No. 5 strips to remaining edges of center unit to complete table topper top. Press seams toward border No. 5.

## finish table topper

**1** Layer table topper top, batting, and backing; baste. (For details, see Complete Quilt, *page 175.*)

**2** Quilt as desired. Diana Johnson machine-quilted a swirly feather design across the table topper top.

**3** Using straight seams, join assorted floral, print, and stripe 2½×5" rectangles to make a pieced binding strip. Bind with pieced binding strip. (For details, see Complete Quilt, *page 175.*)

# back·to
# basics

Refer to these tips and
techniques whenever
you need information
for your projects.

# tools

Before you begin a quilting project, collect the tools and materials you'll need in one easy-to-access place. Below is a list of general supplies.

## FOR CUTTING AND MARKING

**Acrylic ruler:** This thick, clear-plastic ruler helps you make perfectly straight cuts with a rotary cutter. Many sizes are available.

**Marking tools:** Use chalk or special fabric markers, as the marks they make are easy to remove after sewing and quilting.

**Rotary cutter and mat:** These tools have revolutionized quilting because you can cut strips, squares, triangles, and diamonds more quickly, efficiently, and accurately with a rotary cutter and mat than with scissors. Always use a rotary cutter with a mat designed specifically for it to protect your work surface and to keep fabric from shifting while you cut.

**Scissors:** You'll need two pairs—one for fabric and another for paper and plastic.

**Quilting stencils/template plastic:** Precut stencils and template plastic can be traced around multiple times without wearing away any edges.

## FOR PIECING

**Iron and ironing board:** Use an iron and ironing board to press seams, which ensures accurate piecing.

**Sewing machine:** A machine with well-adjusted tension will produce pucker-free patchwork.

### BASIC TOOLS
1. Rotary-cutting mat
2. Template plastic
3. Template
4. Acrylic rulers
5. Chalk marker
6. Marking pencil
7. Water-erasable marker
8. Rotary cutter
9. Bias bars
10. Quilting stencils

**Thread:** There are conflicting opinions about the best thread content. The traditional choice for piecing cotton quilts is 100% cotton thread.

However, with today's thread technology, another option is fine-weight polyester. Quilters must decide for themselves which kind to use.

## SEWING MACHINE NEEDLES

The notions wall in your local quilt shop or sewing center can be intimidating if you're not sure what you need. There are dozens of sizes and shapes of sewing machine needles, each designed for a different task. Understanding the terminology associated with machine needles can take the mystery out of making your selection and make your piecing and quilting go smoother.

**Machine needle sizes:** When looking at a package of machine needles, you will often see two numbers separated by a slash mark. The number on the left of the slash is the European size (range of 60–120); the right-hand number is the American size (range of 8–21). Sizes 70/10, 80/12, and 90/14 are most commonly used for quilting. A lower number indicates a finer machine needle.

**Machine needle points:** The needle point differentiates the type and purpose of a needle and is a key characteristic to consider when selecting a needle for a project. The needle point should match the fabric type. For sewing on quilting cotton, for example, use a needle labeled as a "sharps."

Needles will last longer when you use 100% cotton fabric and batting. Polyester or polyester/cotton blend batting tends to dull needles quicker.

**Machine needle eyes:** The eye width of a needle is about 40% the width of the shaft. A wider shaft means a wider eye. While a needle's eye must be large enough for the thread to pass through with minimal friction, if the eye is too large for the thread, it may produce a seam that is loose and weak. Large needles make large holes, so use the smallest needle appropriate for the thread. Some needles have eyes specially shaped for certain thread types, such as metallic threads, to minimize breakage.

**Machine needle types:** Sharps are the preferred needle type for piecing and quilting woven fabrics such as cotton. They have a very slim point, well-suited for precise straight stitching and topstitching. Sharps needles come in a variety of sizes and brands.

Universal needles can be used on both woven and knit fabrics but are not ideal for piecing because the needle points are slightly rounded. Choose this needle type if you want versatility when working with different fabrics. Metallic needles are designed for use with metallic threads. A larger needle eye accommodates the thread, which tends to be fragile yet rough enough to create burrs in the eye of the needle. Burrs can cause the thread to fray and break.

Topstitch needles can handle heavier decorative threads but also leave larger holes in the fabric.

Specialty needles include double or triple needles, leather needles, jeans needles, embroidery needles, and heirloom-sewing needles. Refer to manufacturers' packaging to determine the needles' best use and thread companion.

## THREAD AND COORDINATING MACHINE NEEDLE SIZES

| | 60/8 | 70/10 | 75/11 | 80/12 | 90/14 |
|---|---|---|---|---|---|
| Piecing and binding cotton fabric with cotton thread | | | ■ | ■ | |
| Piecing flannel | | | | | ■ |
| Quilting with monofilament thread | ■ | ■ | ■ | ■ | |
| Machine appliqué | ■ | ■ | | | |
| Sewing batiks, silks, or high-thread-count fabrics with cotton thread | | ■ | | | |
| Embellishing with decorative threads | | | | ■ | ■ |
| Adding binding and borders | | | ■ | ■ | |

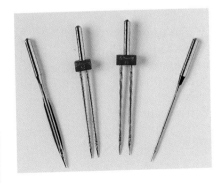

### FOR APPLIQUÉ

**Fusible web:** Use this iron-on adhesive to secure appliqué shapes to a foundation instead of basting with needle and thread.

**Needles:** For hand appliqué, try a fine sharps or milliner's needle.

### FOR HAND QUILTING

**Frame or hoop:** You'll get smaller, more even stitches if you keep your quilt stretched as you stitch. A frame supports the quilt's weight, ensures even tension, and frees both your hands for stitching. Once set up, however, it cannot be disassembled until quilting is complete. Hoops are more portable and less expensive. Quilting hoops are deeper than embroidery hoops to accommodate the thickness of quilt layers.

**Needles:** A "between" or quilting needle is short with a small eye. Common sizes are 8, 9, and 10; size 8 is best for beginners.

**Thimble:** This finger cover relieves the pressure required to push a needle through several layers of fabric and batting.

**Thread:** Quilting thread, including the preferred 100% cotton variety, is stronger than sewing thread.

### FOR MACHINE QUILTING

**Darning, free-motion quilting, or hopper foot:** This sewing machine attachment is used for free-motion quilting. You may find one in your machine's accessory kit. If not, know the model and brand name of your machine when you go to purchase one.

**Safety pins:** Use these pins to hold together a quilt's layers during quilting.

**Table or other large work surface that's level with your machine bed:** Your quilt will need the support.

**Thread:** Look for quilting thread made of either 100% cotton or a cotton-polyester blend. For quilting that blends into the background, use fine nylon or polyester monofilament thread.

**Walking or even-feed foot:** This sewing machine attachment helps you keep long, straight quilting lines smooth and pucker-free.

## choose fabrics

The best fabric for quiltmaking is 100% cotton because it minimizes seam distortion, presses crisply, and is easy to quilt. Unless otherwise noted, quantities in materials lists are for 44/45"-wide fabrics. We call for a little extra yardage to allow for minor cutting errors and slight shrinkage.

## prepare fabrics

There are conflicting opinions about the need to prewash fabric. The debate is a modern one because most antique quilts were made with unwashed fabric. However, today's dyes and sizing are unlike those used a century ago.

Prewashing fabric offers certainty as its main advantage. Today's fabrics resist bleeding and shrinkage, but some of both can occur in some fabrics. Some quilters find prewashed fabric easier to quilt. If you choose to prewash your fabric, press it well before cutting.

Others prefer the crispness of unwashed fabric for machine piecing. If you use fabrics with the same fiber content throughout the quilt, then any shrinkage that occurs in its first washing should be uniform. Some quilters find this small amount of shrinkage

desirable because it gives the quilt a slightly puckered, antique look.

## plan for cutting

This book's instructions list pieces in the order in which they should be cut to make the best use of your fabrics. Always consider the fabric grain before cutting. The arrow on a pattern piece or template indicates which direction the fabric grain should run. One or more straight sides of the pattern piece or template should follow the fabric's lengthwise or crosswise grain.

The lengthwise grain, parallel to the selvage (the tightly finished edge), has the least amount of stretch. (Do not use the selvage of a woven fabric in a quilt. When washed, it may shrink more than the rest of the fabric.) Crosswise grain, perpendicular to the selvage, has a little more give. The edge of any pattern piece that will be on the outside of a block or quilt should always be cut on the lengthwise grain. Be sure to press the fabric before cutting to remove any wrinkles or folds.

## rotary cutting

When cutting, keep an even pressure on the rotary cutter and make sure the blade is touching the edge of the ruler. The less you move your fabric when cutting, the more accurate you'll be.

### SQUARING UP THE FABRIC EDGE

Before rotary-cutting fabric into strips, it is imperative that one fabric edge be made straight, or squared up. Since all subsequent cuts will be measured from this straight edge, squaring up the fabric edge is an important step.

There are several techniques for squaring up an edge, some of which involve the use of a pair of rulers. For clarity and simplicity, we have chosen to describe a single-ruler technique here. *Note:* The instructions are for right-handers.

1. Lay your fabric on the rotary mat with the right side down and one selvage edge away from you. Fold the fabric with the wrong side inside and the selvages together. Fold the fabric in half again, lining up the fold with the selvage edges. Lightly hand-crease all of the folds.

2. Position the folded fabric on the cutting mat with the selvage edges away from you and the bulk of the fabric length to your left. With the ruler on top of the fabric, align a horizontal grid line on the ruler with the lower folded fabric edge, leaving about 1" of fabric exposed along the ruler's right-hand edge (**Photo 1**). Do not worry about or try to align the uneven raw edges along the right-hand side of the fabric. *Note:* If the grid lines on the cutting mat interfere with your ability to focus on the ruler grid lines, turn your cutting mat over and work on the unmarked side.

3. Hold the ruler firmly in place with your left hand, keeping your fingers away from the right-hand edge and spreading your fingers apart slightly. Apply pressure to the ruler with your fingertips to prevent it from slipping as you cut. With the ruler firmly in place, hold the rotary cutter so the blade is touching the right-

PHOTO 1

PHOTO 2

hand edge of the ruler. Roll the blade along the ruler edge, beginning just off the folded edge and pushing the cutter away from you, toward the selvage edge.

4. The fabric strip to the right of the ruler's edge should be cut cleanly away, leaving you with a straight edge from which you can measure all subsequent cuts. Do not pick up the fabric once the edge is squared; instead, turn the cutting mat to rotate the fabric and begin cutting strips.

## CUTTING AND SUBCUTTING STRIPS

To use a rotary cutter to its greatest advantage, first cut a strip of fabric, then subcut the strip into specific sizes. For example, if your instructions say to cut forty 2" squares, follow these steps.

1. First cut a 2"-wide strip crosswise on the fabric. Assuming you have squared up the fabric edge as described earlier, you can turn your cutting mat clockwise 180° with the newly squared-up edge on your left and the excess fabric on the right. Place the ruler on top of the fabric.

2. Align the 2" grid mark on the ruler with the squared-up edge of the fabric (**Photo 2**). *Note:* Align only the vertical grid mark and the fabric raw edge; ignore the selvages at the lower edge that may not line up perfectly with the horizontal ruler grid. A good rule of thumb to remember when rotary-cutting fabric is "the piece you want to keep should be under the ruler." That way, if you accidentally swerve away from the ruler when cutting, the piece under the ruler will be "safe."

3. Placing your rotary cutter along the ruler's right-hand edge and holding the ruler firmly with your left hand, run the blade along the ruler, as in Step 3 of Squaring Up the Fabric Edge, left, to cut the strip. Remove the ruler.

4. Sliding the excess fabric out of the way, carefully turn the mat so the 2" strip is horizontal in relation to you. Refer to Squaring Up the Fabric Edge to trim off the selvage edges and square up the strip's short edges.

PHOTO 3

PHOTO 4

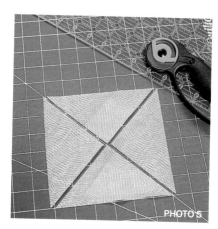

PHOTO 5

**5** Align the ruler's 2" grid mark with a squared-up short edge of the strip (the 2" square you want to keep should be under the ruler). Hold the ruler with your left hand and run the rotary cutter along the right-hand ruler edge to cut a 2" square. To cut multiple 2" squares from one strip, slide the ruler over 2" from the previous cutting line and cut again (**Photo 3**). From a 44/45"-wide strip, you'll likely be able to cut twenty-one 2" squares. Since in this example you need a total of 40, cut a second 2"-wide strip and subcut it into 2" squares.

### CUTTING TRIANGLES

Right triangles also can be quickly and accurately cut with a rotary cutter. There are two common ways to cut triangles. An example of each method follows.

To cut two triangles from one square, the instructions may read:

**From green print, cut:**
- 20—3" squares, cutting each in half diagonally for 40 triangles total

**1** Referring to Cutting and Subcutting Strips, beginning on *page 169*, cut a 3"-wide

fabric strip and subcut the strip into 3" squares.

**2** Line up the ruler's edge with opposite corners of a square to cut it in half diagonally (**Photo 4**). Cut along the ruler's edge. *Note:* The triangles' resultant long edges are on the bias. Avoid stretching or overhandling these edges when piecing so that seams don't become wavy and distorted.

To cut four triangles from one square, the instructions may read:

**From green print, cut:**
- 20—6" squares, cutting each diagonally twice in an X for 80 triangles total

**3** Referring to Cutting and Subcutting Strips, beginning on *page 169*, cut a 6"-wide fabric strip and subcut it into 6" squares.

**4** Line up the ruler's edge with opposite corners of a square to cut it in half diagonally. Cut along the ruler's edge; do not separate the two triangles created. Line up the ruler's edge with the remaining corners and cut along the

ruler's edge to make a total of four triangles (**Photo 5**). *Note:* The triangles' resultant short edges are on the bias. Avoid stretching or overhandling these edges when piecing so that seams don't become wavy and distorted.

## cut bias strips

Strips for curved appliqué pieces and for binding curved edges should be cut on the bias (diagonally across the grain of a woven fabric), which runs at a 45° angle to the selvage and has the most stretch.

To cut bias strips, begin with a fabric square or rectangle; use an acrylic ruler to square up the left edge if necessary. Make a cut at a 45° angle to the left edge (**Bias Strip Diagram**). Handle the diagonal edges carefully to avoid distorting the bias. To cut a strip, measure the desired width from the 45° cut edge; cut parallel to the edge. Cut enough strips to total the length needed.

**BIAS STRIP DIAGRAM**

# make and use templates

## MAKE TEMPLATE

A template is a pattern made from extra-sturdy material so you can trace around it many times without wearing away the edges. Acrylic templates for many common shapes are available at quilt shops. Or make your own by duplicating printed patterns on template plastic.

To make permanent templates, purchase easy-to-cut template plastic, available at quilt shops and crafts supply stores. Lay the plastic over a printed pattern. Trace the pattern onto the plastic using a ruler and a permanent marker to ensure straight lines, accurate corners, and permanency.

For hand piecing and appliqué, make templates the exact size the finished pieces will be (without seam allowances). For piecing, this means tracing the patterns' dashed lines.

For machine piecing, make templates that include seam allowances by tracing the patterns' solid and dashed lines onto the template plastic.

For easy reference, mark each template with its letter designation, grain line (if noted on the pattern), and block or quilt name. Also mark the matching point of each corner on the seam line (these may be indicated with dots on the printed pattern). Cut out the traced shapes on their outside lines. Using a pushpin, make a hole in the template at each corner matching point. The hole must be large enough for the point of a pencil or marking pen to mark through.

Verify each template's shape and size by placing it over its printed pattern. Templates must be accurate because errors, however small, compound many times as you assemble a quilt. To check templates' accuracy, make a test block before cutting the fabric pieces for an entire quilt.

## USE TEMPLATES

To trace a template on fabric, use a pencil, a white dressmaker's pencil, chalk, or a special fabric marker that makes a thin, accurate line. Do not use a ballpoint or ink pen; the lines may bleed if washed. Test all marking tools on a fabric scrap before using them.

To make pieces for hand piecing, place a template facedown on the wrong side of the fabric and trace. If desired, mark the matching points on the corners of the seam lines. Reposition the template at least ½" away from the previous tracing, trace again, and repeat (Diagram 1). To make pieces for hand appliqué, place a template faceup on the right side of the fabric and trace. The lines you trace on the fabric are the sewing lines. Mark cutting lines ¼" away from the sewing lines, or estimate the distance by eye when cutting out the pieces with scissors. For hand piecing, add a ¼" seam allowance; for hand appliqué, add a ³⁄₁₆" seam allowance.

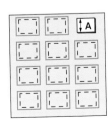

**DIAGRAM 1**

Because templates used to make pieces for machine piecing have seam allowances included, you can use common tracing lines for efficient cutting. Place a template facedown on the wrong side of the fabric and trace. Mark the corner matching points through the holes in the template; each one should be right on the seam line. Reposition the template without leaving a space between it and the previous tracing, trace again, and repeat (Diagram 2). Using a rotary cutter and ruler, cut out pieces, cutting precisely on the drawn lines.

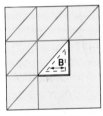

**DIAGRAM 2**

## PLAN FOR CUTTING

Our project instructions list pieces in the order they should be cut to make the best use of your fabrics.

Always consider the fabric grain before cutting. The arrow on a pattern piece indicates which direction the grain should run. One or more straight edges of a pattern piece should follow the fabric's lengthwise or crosswise grain.

The lengthwise grain, parallel to the selvages (the tightly finished edges), has the least amount of stretch. The crosswise grain, perpendicular to the selvages, has a little more give. The edge of any pattern piece that will be on the outside of a block or quilt should be cut on the lengthwise grain.

Do not use the selvage of a woven fabric in a quilt. When washed, it may shrink more than the rest of the fabric.

In projects larger than 42" in length or width, we usually specify that the border strips be cut the width (crosswise grain) of the fabric and pieced to use the least amount of fabric. If you'd prefer to cut the border strips on the lengthwise grain and not piece them, you'll need to refigure the yardage.

## machine piecing

Machine piecing depends on sewing an exact ¼" seam allowance. Some machines have a presser foot that is the proper width, or a ¼" foot is available. To check the width of a machine's presser foot, sew a sample seam with the raw fabric edges aligned with the right edge of the presser foot; measure the resultant seam allowance using graph paper with a ¼" grid.

Using two thread colors— one in the needle and one in the bobbin—can help you to better match your thread color to your fabrics. If your quilt has many fabrics, use a neutral color, such as gray or beige, for both the top and bobbin threads throughout the quilt.

## press for success

In quilting, almost every seam needs to be pressed before the piece is sewn to another, so keep your iron and ironing board near your sewing area. It's important to remember to press with an up and down motion. Moving the iron around on the fabric can distort seams, especially those sewn on the bias.

Project instructions in this book generally tell you in what direction to press each seam. When in doubt, press the seam allowance toward the darker fabric. When joining rows of blocks, alternate the direction the seam allowances are pressed to ensure flat corners.

## set in seams

The key to sewing angled pieces together (setting in seams) is carefully aligning marked matching points. Here, we use diamonds and a square—a common type of set-in seam—to illustrate the process. Whether you're stitching by machine or by hand, start and stop sewing precisely at the matching points (dots on **Diagram 3**); be sure to backstitch to secure seam ends.

### BY MACHINE

First make an angled unit by sewing two diamonds together between matching points along a pair of edges (**Diagram 3**).

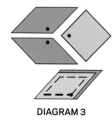

**DIAGRAM 3**

Then, with right sides together, pin one edge of the angled unit to one edge of the square (**Diagram 4**). Align matching points at either end, pushing a pin through both fabric layers to check alignment. Machine-stitch precisely between matching points, backstitching at seam ends. Remove unit from sewing machine.

**DIAGRAM 4**

Bring adjacent edge of angled unit up and align it with the next edge of the square (**Diagram 5**). Insert a pin in each corner to align matching points as before. Machine-stitch between matching points. Press seams away from set-in piece (the square).

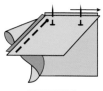

**DIAGRAM 5**

### BY HAND

First make an angled unit by sewing two diamonds together between matching points along a pair of edges (**Diagram 3**).

Then, with right sides together, pin one edge of the angled unit to an edge of the square (**Diagram 6**). Use pins to align matching points.

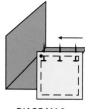

**DIAGRAM 6**

Hand-sew the seam from the open end of the angled unit to the matching point in the corner. Remove pins as you sew and backstitch at the corner to secure stitches. Do not sew into the ¼" seam allowance, and do not cut your thread.

Bring the adjacent edge of the square up and align it with the next edge of the angled unit. Insert a pin in each corner to align matching points as before, then pin remainder of the seam (Diagram 7). Hand-sew seam from inside corner to open end of the angle, removing pins as you sew. Press seams away from set-in piece (the square).

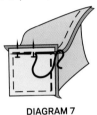

DIAGRAM 7

PHOTO 6

PHOTO 7

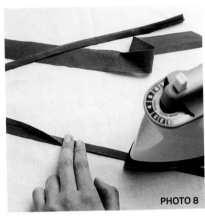

PHOTO 8

PHOTO 9

# appliqué

We encourage beginners to select an appliqué design with straight lines and gentle curves. Learning to make sharp points and tiny stitches takes practice.

In the following instructions, we've used a stemmed flower motif as the appliqué example.

### BASTE THE SEAM ALLOWANCES

Begin by turning under the $3/16$" seam allowances on the appliqué pieces; press. Some quilters like to thread-baste the folded edges to ensure proper placement. Edges that will be covered by other pieces don't need to be turned under.

For sharp points on tips, first trim the seam allowance to within $1/8$" of the stitching line (Photo 6), tapering the sides gradually to $3/16$". Fold under the seam allowance remaining on the tips. Then turn the seam allowances under on both sides of the tips. The side seam allowances will overlap slightly at the tips, forming sharp points.

Baste the folded edges in place (Photo 7). The turned seam allowances may form little pleats on the back side that you also should baste in place. Remove the basting stitches after the shapes have been appliquéd to the foundation.

### MAKE BIAS STEMS

For graceful curves, cut appliqué stems on the bias. The strips for stems can be prepared in various ways. Heat-resistant bias bars may be purchased in a size to match the desired finished width of the bias tube you wish to make. They are a handy tool for making appliqué stems.

For an alternate method, fold and press the strip in half, then fold the raw edges to meet at the center; press in half again as shown in Photo 8. Or fold the bias strip in half lengthwise with the wrong side inside; press. Stitch $1/4$" from the raw edges to keep them aligned. Fold the strip in half again, hiding the raw edges behind the first folded edge; press.

### POSITION AND STITCH

Pin the prepared appliqué pieces in place on the foundation (Photo 9) using the position markings or referring to the appliqué placement diagram. If your pattern suggests it, mark the position for each piece on the foundation before you begin. Overlap the flowers and stems as indicated.

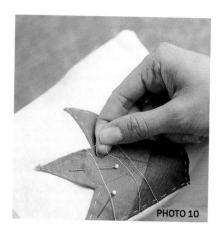

PHOTO 10

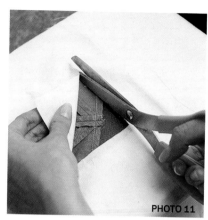

PHOTO 11

Using thread in colors that match the fabrics, sew each stem and blossom onto the foundation with small slip stitches as shown in **Photo 10**. (For photographic purposes, thread color does not match fabric color.)

Catch only a few threads of the stem or flower fold with each stitch. Pull the stitches taut, but not so tight that they pucker the fabric. You can use the needle's point to manipulate the appliqué edges as needed. Take an extra slip stitch at the point of a petal to secure it to the foundation.

You can use hand-quilting needles for appliqué stitching, but some quilters prefer a longer milliner's or straw needle. The extra needle length aids in tucking fabric under before taking slip stitches.

If the foundation fabric shows through the appliqué fabrics, cut away the foundation fabric. Trimming the foundation fabric also reduces the bulk of multiple layers when quilting later. Carefully trim the underlying fabric to within ¼" of the appliqué stitches (**Photo 11**) and avoid cutting the appliqué fabrics.

### FUSIBLE APPLIQUÉ
For quick-finish appliqué, use paper-backed lightweight fusible web. You can iron the shapes onto the foundation and add decorative stitching to the edges. This product consists of two layers, a fusible webbing lightly bonded to paper that peels off. The webbing adds a slight stiffness to appliqué pieces.

When purchasing this product, read the directions on the package to make sure you're buying the right kind for your project. Some are specifically engineered to bond fabrics with no sewing at all. If you try to stitch fabric after it has bonded with one of these products, you may have difficulty. Some paper-backed fusible products are made only for sewn edges; others work with or without stitching.

If you buy paper-backed fusible web from a bolt, be sure fusing instructions are included because the iron temperature and timing vary by brand. This information is usually on the paper backing.

With any of these products, the general procedure is to trace the patterns wrong side up onto the paper side of the fusible web. Then place the fusible-web pieces on the wrong side of the appliqué fabrics, paper side up, and use an iron to fuse the layers together. Cut out the fabric shapes, peel off the paper, turn the fabrics right side up, and fuse them to the foundation fabric.

You also can fuse the fusible web and fabric together before tracing. You'll still need to trace templates wrong side up on the paper backing.

If you've used a no-sew fusible web, your appliqué is done. If not, finish the edges with hand or machine stitching.

## miter borders
To add a border with mitered corners, first pin a border strip to one edge of the quilt top, matching centers. Sew together, beginning and ending seam ¼" from quilt top corners (**Diagram 8**). Allow excess border fabric to extend beyond edges of quilt top. Repeat with remaining border strips. Press seams toward border strips.

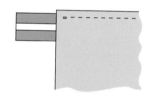

DIAGRAM 8

At a corner, lap one border strip over the other (**Diagram 9**). Align the edge of a 90° triangle with the raw edge of the top strip so that the long edge of the triangle intersects the border seam in the corner. With a pencil, draw along edge of triangle from seam out to the raw edge. Place bottom border strip on top and repeat the marking process.

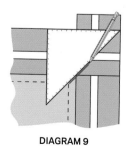

DIAGRAM 9

With right sides together, match marked seam lines and pin (Diagram 10). Beginning with a backstitch at the inside corner, sew together strips, stitching exactly on marked lines. Check the right side to make sure corner lies flat. Trim excess fabric, leaving a ¼" seam allowance. Press seam open. Mark and sew remaining corners in the same manner.

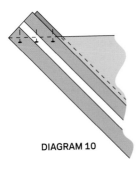

DIAGRAM 10

## select batting

For a small beginner project, a thin cotton batting is a good choice. It tends to stick to fabric, so it requires less basting. Also, it's easy to stitch. It's wise to follow the stitch density recommendation printed on the packaging; this indicates the maximum distance between rows of stitching required to keep the batting from shifting and wadding up inside the quilt.

Polyester batting is lightweight and readily available. In general, it springs back to its original height when it is compressed, adding a puffiness to quilts. It tends to "beard" (work out between the weave of the fabric) more than natural fibers. Polyester fleece is denser than polyester batting and works well for pillow tops and place mats.

Wool batting has good loft retention and absorbs moisture, making it ideal for cool, damp climates. Read the label carefully before purchasing a wool batting; it may require special handling.

## complete quilt

Cut and piece backing fabric to measure at least 4" bigger on all sides than the quilt top. Press seams open. With wrong sides together, layer quilt top and backing fabric with batting in between; baste. Quilt as desired.

Binding for most quilts is cut on the straight grain of the fabric. If your quilt has curved edges, cut binding strips on the bias. Cutting instructions for the projects in this issue specify the number of binding strips or a total length needed to finish the quilt. Instructions also specify enough width for a French-fold, or double-layer, binding because it's easier to apply and adds durability.

Join strips with diagonal seams to make one continuous binding strip (Diagram 11). Trim excess fabric, leaving ¼" seam allowances. Press seams open. Fold one end of the binding strip under 1" (Diagram 12); press.

DIAGRAM 11

DIAGRAM 12

DIAGRAM 13

With wrong side inside, fold strip in half lengthwise and press (Diagram 13).

Beginning in center of one edge, place binding strip against right side of quilt top, aligning binding strip's raw edges with quilt top's raw edge (Diagram 14). Sew through all layers, stopping ¼" (or a distance equal to the seam allowance you're using) from the corner. Backstitch, then clip threads. Remove quilt from under the sewing-machine presser foot.

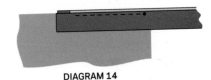

DIAGRAM 14

Fold binding strip upward, creating a diagonal fold, and finger-press (Diagram 15).

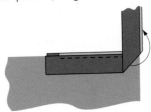

DIAGRAM 15

Holding diagonal fold in place with your finger, bring binding strip down in line with next edge of quilt top, making a horizontal fold that aligns with the quilt edge (Diagram 16).

DIAGRAM 16

Start sewing again at top of horizontal fold, stitching through all layers. Sew around quilt, turning each corner in same manner.

When you return to the starting point, encase binding strip's raw edge inside the folded end (Diagram 17). Finish sewing to the starting point (Diagram 18). Trim batting and backing fabric even with the quilt top edges.

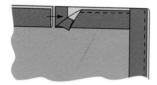

**DIAGRAM 17**

**DIAGRAM 18**

Turn binding over each edge to the back. Hand-stitch binding to backing fabric, making sure to cover all machine stitching.

To make mitered corners on the back, hand-stitch up to a corner; fold a miter in the binding. Take a stitch or two in the fold to secure it. Then stitch the binding in place up to the next corner. Finish each corner in the same manner.

# hanging sleeves

Quilts make wonderful pieces of wall art. When treated as museum pieces and hung properly, they won't deteriorate. Let size be your guide when determining how to hang your quilt.

Hang smaller quilts, a 25" square or less, with purchased clips, sewn-on tabs, or pins applied to the corners. Larger quilts require a hanging sleeve

attached to the back. It may take a few minutes more to sew on a sleeve, but the effort preserves your hours of work with less distortion and damage.

## MAKE A HANGING SLEEVE

1 Measure the quilt's top edge.

2 Cut a 6"- to 10"-wide strip of prewashed fabric 2" longer than the quilt's top edge. For example, if the top edge is 40", cut a 6×42" strip. A 6"-wide strip is sufficient for a dowel or drapery rod. If you're using something bigger in diameter, cut a wider fabric strip. If you're sending your quilt to be displayed at a quilt show, adjust your measurements to accommodate the show's requirements.

3 Fold under 1½" on both ends of the fabric strip. Sew ¼" from the raw edges (Diagram 19).

**DIAGRAM 19**

4 Fold the fabric strip in half lengthwise with the wrong side inside; pin. Stitch together the long edges with a ¼" seam allowance (Diagram 20) to make the sleeve. Press seam allowance open and center the seam in the middle of the sleeve (Diagram 21).

**DIAGRAM 20**

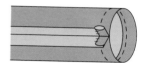

**DIAGRAM 21**

5 Center the sleeve on the quilt back about 1" below the binding with the seam facing the back (Diagram 22). Slip-stitch the sleeve to the quilt along both long edges and the portions of the short edges that touch the back, stitching through the back and batting.

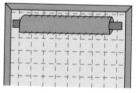

**DIAGRAM 22**

6 Slide a wooden dowel or slender piece of wood that is 1" longer than the finished sleeve into the sleeve and hang as desired.